NO WATER

IN

MY CUP

EXPERIENCES AND A CONTROLLED STUDY

OF

PSYCHOTHERAPY OF DELINQUENT GIRLS

RATIBOR-RAY M. JURJEVICH, Ph.D.
Clinical Psychologist

Foreword by
O. Hobart Mowrer, Ph.D.
Research Professor of Psychology

LIBRA PUBLISHERS, INC.

© 1968 by Libra Publishers, Inc.

FIRST EDITION

Published by Libra Publishers, Inc.
1133 Broadway, New York, N. Y. 10010

Manufactured in the United States of America

Library of Congress Catalog Card No.: 68-9415

CONTENTS

Dora's Poem "No Water in My Cup"   iii
Acknowledgments   vi
Foreword   vii
Introduction   9
  A failure of insight therapy   10
  Insight demoted   26
  Uniqueness of every psychotherapy   28
  The therapist and the method   29
  The institutional training   33
  Two precursors   35

Part I

What We Said and did:
Girls and Their Reactions in Psychotherapy

Ann   43
Betty   46
Cora   50
Dora   54
Emma   61
Fay   67
Grace   69
Hanna   73
Judy   79
Kate   83
Lou   87
Mary   89
Nora   95
Olga   97
Comments   105

Part II — Research report

Introduction: Uncertainties about effects of psychotherapy   113
Tables   120
Problem   121

Methods and procedures   121
    Basic design   121
    Selection of subjects   121
    Psychotherapeutic method   123
    The therapist   129
    Instruments of evaluation   130
Results   134
Discussion of results   146
Conclusions   150
Follow-up study   153
Summary   155
References   156

APPENDICES

  I   Questionnaire regarding the interest in individual psy-
      chotherapy   163
  II   The rationale of the Rorschach hypotheses   164
 III   The additional Rorschach Content Test scoring items   167
 IV   Self and Ideal Self Sort: Development, instructions,
      items   168
  V   Psychological meaning of the 16 Personality Factor
      traits   177
 VI   Additional matching criteria   183
VII   Rating schedule of parole adjustment   184

To Our Mother

who raised us by her loving example

No Water in My Cup

I feel like the world is falling in on me.
Oh, if I could only be free!
But if I should find no water in my cup,
I know I will never give up!

I'll try to do best of all,
And try my best not to fall.
I'll put that water in my cup,
Because I'll never ever give up.

I'll try my best to help everyone,
Where there is darkness I'll bring the sun.
And when hardships seem to follow me,
I'll think of happy things in all I see.
Then, with water overflowing in my cup,
My heart will say: "You Never Gave Up."

Dora, struggling in therapy

Acknowledgments

Although I remain responsible for any shoctcomings of this report, many people have contributed to various phases of the research. Without their good will, I could not have accomplished the task.

The Superintendent of the then State Training School for Girls, now Mountview School for Girls, Miss Betty Portner not only authorized the research, but also encouraged the cooperation of other staff members of the Institution by her continued interest. The teachers and counselors never begrudged the time given to ratings of the experimental and control subjects. Miss Betty Heshion, the patient secretary of the Social Service Department, spent many hours in administering, scoring and tabulating the tests.

The writer is indebted to his colleagues Drs. Bonnie Webb Camp, E. Ellis Graham, B. Lynn Harriman, Walter Limbacher and Don Loy for critically reading an early form of the manuscript and suggesting a number of necessary improvements. Mr. Don Krill gave substantial help in smoothing out the inadequate English constructions of the first draft of the Introduction and of Part I. The final text was ably edited by Mrs. Marlene Chambers. My office helpers, Airmen Darrel D. Naasz and Elliot J. Sidey, contributed willingly to the work on the final text of the book.

A recognition is extended here to Mr. Richard S. Douglas, Director, Division of Juvenile Parole, state of Colorado, and to his staff members who readily responded to the writer's request for ratings of the girls on parole. Thanks are also due to Mrs. Bonnie Geer who took part in the follow-up ratings.

Grateful acknowledgment is given to the International Universities Press, Inc. for permission to quote from B. H. Balser's *Psychotherapy of Adolescents* and from K. R. Eissler's *Searchlights of Delinquency*: to Dr. R. B. Cattell for allowing the inclusion in this report of the factor descriptions of his "16 Personality Factor Questionnaires; to Dr. W. Glasser for extracts of his address on Reality Therapy; to Harper and Brothers for quotations from *Mental Health or Mental Illness* by W. Glasser; to *American Journal of Psychiatry* for quotation from Dr. I. Stevenson's article.

FOREWORD

For the field of clinical psychology, the past decade has been an era of unrest, upheaval, and radical change. What seemed to be unshakable orthodoxies have crumbled, and previously unthinkable innovations have found widespread, if tentative, acceptance. The present volume tells an important part of this story of revolution and evolution.

Ideas and ideological change are not, of course, disembodied, impersonal phenomena. They are part and parcel of human experience and, in the final analysis, occur in and are mediated by individuals. The sequence of events which unfolds in this book therefore involves not only an intellectual and professional reorientation, but also an account, by the author, of personal frustration, challenge, and redirection. The book is, in fact, a sort of "diary," with both personal and professional dimensions. As such, it constitutes a chapter or stage in an on-going, developing process and progression, the end of which is by no means as yet in sight.

Paradoxically, some of the most important developments in this whole area have come from failure and, very recently, success in the treatment of "untreatables." Classical psychoanalysis and many derivative therapeutic systems have taken an ambiguous position with respect to so-called "character disorders," as opposed to the "psychoneuroses." On the one hand, there has been a tendency to put these two personality types into opposing categories: individuals with delinquent, criminal, acting-out, or "character" problems, i.e., sociopaths, were assumed to be *under*-socialized, whereas neurotic and functionally psychotic persons were assumed to be *over*-socialized. In the one case, there was presumed to be a personality or character *deficit*—in the other, a personality *excess;* and since psychoanalysis and associated procedures are primarily surgical or subtractive, at least in intent if not effect, they were manifestly applicable only to persons with characterological excess, namely, neurotics. Sociopaths, because they were presumed to have a characterological deficit, were therefore commonly dismissed as "untreatable."

On the other hand, there has also been a widespread tendency, in the same psychotherapeutic circles, to assume that delinquents are no less conflicted and "sick" than are neurotics and that the difference is simply, or at least mainly, one of symptom choice: the delinquent's symptoms typically involve "acting-out" whereas the neurotic's symptoms typically involve "anxiety." And those who have taken this second view of the matter have often set out to "treat" sociopaths by using the same procedures as were assumed to be effective with neurotic persons.

But eventually it became evident that the "treatment approach" to the problem of sociopathy which had been dictated by psychodynamic principles was not working—and was not likely to work—as indicated, for example, in Lee R. Steiner's 1960 book *Understanding the Juvenile Delinquent*. And gradually it became apparent that this approach was not even working where it was supposed to work best: namely, with psychoneurotic persons (see reviews by Eysenck, 1961, and by Mowrer, 1968). Then, remarkably enough, reports began to appear of success in the rehabilitation of hard-core delinquents (Glasser, 1965) and drug addicts (Casriel, 1962; Yablonsky, 1965; Shelly & Bassin, 1965; Casriel & Deitch, 1966). The "untreatables" had become treatable —but only because so-called treatment had ceased to be treatment in the conventional sense of the term, and had become something different. Now methods of re-education—involving intensive, demanding, but loving interaction between persons, in a broadly family-type atmosphere—are producing results which classical forms of psychotherapy and rehabilitation never even approximated. Dr. Jurjevich's *No Water in My Cup* is part of this breakthrough, this discovery that youthful as well as more seasoned sociopaths *can* be successfully and dramatically changed, a fact which is now, paradoxically, beginning to bring new hope and a new perspective to the entire field of psychotherapy.

Dr. Jurjevich describes the process whereby he moved from the kind of "insight" therapy he had been taught as a graduate student to a new emphasis on present behavior and its modification, by means of special attention to feelings and interpersonal relationships. What emerges is a form of "relationship therapy," which is patently an advance over the detachment and purely intellectual interest of therapists of a former day. What is perhaps most crucially missing here is the implementation of this approach in a *group* setting, where members participate as both patients and therapists—or, more precisely, as both students and as teachers. In the work of Jurjevich and of Glasser, however advanced it is in many respects, there is still a dichotomy between professionals and laymen, between staff and inmates. The genius of the the self-help programs such as those of Synanon Foundation and Daytop Village, Inc. (see references already cited) lies in the fact that here this distinction is obliterated, with an even more striking gain in effectiveness (cf. Glasser & Iverson, 1967). The professional, it seems, still has a place in rehabilitation work; but it is mainly that of helping set up self-help programs and then giving them maximal support and minimal supervision.

This book looks in decidedly the right direction. And readers will find it very helpful in making the transition, in their thinking and their practice, from traditional conceptions of sociopathy in particular and psychopathology in general to the new and radically different forms of personality alteration which have now achieved a high level of proficiency in the self-help approaches and programs here cited. Ray Jurjevich is to be congratulated on his pioneering work in this field, and thanked for so candidly and courageously sharing his personal experiences and professional findings.

O. Hobart Mowrer, Ph. D.
Research Professor of Psychology
University of Illinois
Urbana, Illinois

INTRODUCTION

The work described in these pages represents in several ways a phase in my professional biography. The study arose out of my uncertainty concerning the usefulness of psychotherapeutic work with delinquents. The experience I have gained in the study shaped my views as to how I can best apply myself in psychotherapy. Also the methods adopted sprang partly from my own experience and development as a person.

When I began this study I was employed as clinical psychologist by the State Training School for Girls (now Mountview School for Girls) in Colorado for more than a year (1958-1959). By choice, and professional belief in the value of psychotherapy I structured my work in such a way that at least half of my working hours were spent in individual interviews.

The lack of progress evident in some girls, or the slowness and apparent instability in the improvement of others raised some disquieting questions. The perusal of literature on effects of psychotherapy (reviewed here at the beginning of Part II), only increased these doubts and uncertainties. I was caught in a dilemma.

On the one hand, there was the faith that psychotherapy has definite stabilizing effects in emotionally troubled persons. There were improvements in personality functioning clinically observed not only by me at the beginning of my career as a psychotherapist, but also by other experienced workers testifying to their faith in a multitude of books and periodicals. On the other hand, there was a dearth of verified results through well controlled studies. I could neither abandon psychotherapy as useless, nor apply myself to it without the gnawing doubt that I might be wasting time in individual interviews which could be used more profitably in some other form of help. I decided that the resolution of these professional tensions could be achieved by undertaking a controlled research.

By that time I had spent over one thousand hours with more than forty girls in the institution. The clinical experiences and observations of that first year of psychotherapy with delinquents led to the formulation of definite rational principles as well as to intuitive hunches about the ingredients important for effective help. I evolved an approach to psychotherapy different from that to which I had been exposed in my graduate training. The main difference lay in abandoning the concept of insight as the main method of facilitating changes in personalities, and placing stronger emphasis on the present behavior, achievement of self-respect, and the responsible adoption and practice of personal values as the basis for inner peace and stability.

A Failure of Insight Therapy

Psychoanalysis and allied procedures placed considerable stress on insight as a means of reorganizing the subject's reactions and feelings. Some fixations in development are expected to be loosened through insight about the origins of pathological reactions and to liberate the subject to proceed toward more wholesome behavior. Interpretation at appropriate times is considered crucial in enabling the subject to change himself. The nondirective theory of therapy also considers self-understanding as an important factor in personality improvement.

I followed these ideas dutifully in the course of my first year of work with delinquents. The experience taught me that I was following an ineffectual method, at least for this delinquent population. Glasser states that "the most common misconception in all psychotherapy is the often fixed idea that therapy consists of the psychiatrist giving insight to the patient. People come to psychiatrists not understanding that it is a defective ego which has made therapy necessary, but rather with the idea that if they knew why they were feeling or acting as they did they would be comfortable. In no other branch of therapeutics, whether medicine, auto repairing, or animal disease is such a 'miracle cure' expected; yet the idea remains steadfastly fixed in peoples' minds about psychiatry and psychotherapy. Here, for reasons perpetuated both by psychiatrists and by many who write about psychiatry, this false idea has come to be almost gospel.

Just finding out what was wrong and how it happened, or even learning what is wrong now, cannot initiate more effective ego functioning. If one has an effective ego, this knowledge may be of great help because in that case the person has the ego to deal with the situation. If not, insight into the defective-ego functioning does not help any more than does the understanding that Sam can't walk because he has a broken leg. This information is good to know, but much correct therapy is needed before Sam can walk. To find that you are frightened of high places because certain important events happened in relation to important people early in your life does not help you get over the fear. Unless the ego is made more effective, the phobia will continue unabated." (Glasser, 1960, pp. 166, 167.)

The following case is offered as an illustration of the feeble effect of insight with delinquents, even when the neurotic symptoms were prominent, and the transference reaction was noticeable. The writer does not mean "transference" in the technical psychoanalytic meaning, but in the broader sense in which Goldstein (1959) conceives it. He calls it rather "communion," "state of solidarity" with the person in treatment; "the feeling of common enterprise," faith and confidence in the therapist. Speaking of the patient-physician relationship in chronic somatic diseases, Goldstein almost summarized the case to be described here: ". . . only if a deeper mutual relationship has been established—if the patient believes that the physician is as deeply involved as he is himself—will the patient continue treatment in the not uncommon cases in which the therapy does not seem to lead to improvement or where the symptoms increase." The case also gives a preview of the difficulties, the setbacks and frustrations involved in the individual psychotherapy of delinquents.

Sandra was sixteen when she asked to see the psychologist. She appeared depressed and irritable, hostile to both adults and peers, and troubled by thoughts of running away—which she knew would be futile, for this was her second stay in the institution. Her mother, an attractive young woman who suffered from ulcers, had returned Sandra to the institution after her first escape. Sandra thought that her troubles started after the death of her grandmother, when she was eleven years old. The grandparents were the only ones who had been good to her, she said.

Sandra had had two previous psychological evaluations at the Diagnostic Center because of truancy, fighting in school and in the neighborhood, roaming the streets, and associating with known delinquents. Since her parents had separated before her birth Sandra had never known her father, who now lives somewhere in the South. She quarreled with her mother constantly. "Mother doesn't get along with anyone in the family. They don't think much of her. When I was younger. I wondered where our money came from. I was stupid. I should have known about it—there were so many men coming to the house. She wanted me to earn my living in the same way. I wouldn't do it for money."

I tried to reinforce this negative identification with the mother.

"You want others to respect you so that you'll feel good within yourself too."

"Yes, I have to keep out of trouble. I am doing it already here. I wanted to hit Mrs. R., but I went to my room to cool off. I can be roguey, but I can stop it too. I can learn useful things here."

"What do you have in mind?"

"To take life as it is, and not always try to make it the way I want it. I can take orders now—to some extent, anyway. I couldn't do that before."

"Do you feel more mature this way?"

"Yes, if I want to."

"So it depends on you what happens to you in your life."

"Yes. That's why we like to see your car in front of our cottage."

"Why is that?"

"When we start getting foolish we can run to you and keep out of trouble."

Apparently Sandra was beginning to separate her impulsive reactions from the more rational and socially appropriate possibilities open to her. I was trying to use her more mature tendencies in helping her and bring into the open the opposition between the regressing and integrating impulses.

Sometimes she liked to sit on the carpet instead of in the chair, with her back turned to me. She said she was so tired, sleepy. "You want to feel like a little girl now, here with me, so I can help you grow up." She denied it. But when I passed her with a group of girls on the grounds she called "Daddy" with a teasing smile. In this way she was publicly denying and confirming her transference reaction.

During one interview, while in her usual somber mood, she said she hated to see her birthday coming. She wanted to stay the way she was. I used the occasion again. "To stay a child. Might that be your real problem, that you are afraid to grow up, so that you sometimes behave childishly?"

"Yes. It has advantages and disadvantages. The advantage if you do not grow is that they don't hold you responsible for what you do. The disadvantage is that if you are a child you are not free to do what you want to. But the adults have to obey the rules too."

"So you can't decide if it's worth growing up?"

"I wonder. But I'll grow up one day."

The movement toward more responsible behavior was initiated. A few days later she told me how she had handled a disagreement with another girl. "I would've gotten into a fight with her before. But now I asked her to talk it over like ladies instead of squabbling like two-year-olds. I hope I'll be able to keep my temper." This was in the thirteenth interview, two months after the beginning of our contact. This girl, considered recalcitrant by the staff members, seemed to be making headway in belated growth. Before leaving the institution on parole, she asked me to keep a snapshot of her "to a very good friend, whom I treasure," and wondered whether she could come for some interviews if she needed them. She did not come, partly because the institution was far out in the country; but often called on the telephone when she felt restless and anxious.

Two months later she was returned to the institution for having violated parole conditions. She had gone back to her wild friends, and the aunt with whom she was placed could not handle her. She was pale and lean, and the nurse had to treat her for a vaginal discharge. She denied having any sexual experience, and even proudly told me how she had broken off with her boy friend when he suggested pimping for her. Apparently, when she was with the therapist she could take up the role dictated by her conscience. She was with a "Daddy" who had not progressed enough in his role to openly disapprove of her return to irresponsibility, so she played the make-believe of her innocence. But soon she had to face a depressive dip in her emotions.

She complained in the following interview: "I do not know what's the matter with me. I'm so mean with people even if they're friendly with me. I'm snotty, mean, just evil."

"What are you unhappy about?"

13

"Don't know what to think. But I'm not my old wild self. Don't want to carry on like I used to. When I went to my aunt's and heard them quarreling and going out on each other, and that messy home, it made me disgusted. She and my mother are just like I used to be, carefree and childish. But I don't know if I like my new self either. I'm very quiet, and I think before I say or do something. I can't talk foolishly with Barb like I used to. I put a distance between us there and a limit—sort of. But I still have nightmares. Last night I dreamed that they were going to lock me up in a place here and I'd never get out. I told them that I came here chasing someone to get my coat back; then a mad dog was trying to bite me and a man saved me, let me in his car."

"Do you feel worried that you are back in the institution? Who might be the mad dog that was chasing you?"

"I was thinking of that boy who proposed marriage to me. I always wanted to have a baby, even when I was small. But maybe later I'll find some other boy I like better."

"What's the hurry? You can't carry out any decision while you're in the school anyway."

She looked up, and smiled as if a load had fallen off her back. "I have to learn not to get wrapped up in my thoughts so much. In fact I think I should finish high school first. I want to go to East High. They don't learn much in my old school."

"You seem to be torn between what might be good for you in the long run and what you might wish for this moment."

She nodded, sighed, smiled, as if getting a grasp of herself. However, she was quite restless during the next several weeks, and came to the interviews talking about her anger with others, of her loneliness. She could "never make friends." Even as a child she had wondered if others liked her for herself or because she had a bike. "How is this connected with your mother?" I asked her.

She kept quiet for a long period of time, then sobbed softly. It was difficult to understand all she was saying. "My mother? She's strange. She's like a teen-ager. She'd ride a motorcycle in jeans, even on a Sunday. Other people asked me if she was my mother, and I'd sort of say, 'yes.' I wonder if she's really my mother. I remember how she took my blanket off me even though the room was cold, and she went with a guy on the porch. She taught me a horrid dance for a strip tease that I did in our home for some airmen. They were older than my father."

14

"It makes you sad that you did not have a mother the way you wanted her to be."

Her shoulders shook from violent sobbing. "No, she never was like a mother. My grandma was my mother, but she died. I've never loved anyone since. I can't let myself. I fooled with fellows, but it wasn't love. I know I love you, but you told me that it was hopeless because you love your wife and you want to remain a counselor to me. I wanted to take care of grandpa. Yesterday I saw a movie and it made me feel hollow all this time. It reminded me so much of grandma. I couldn't stop crying and wouldn't believe she was dead."

In this interview, and in later ones, many interpretations were made: that she hoped to obtain from others the love she missed in her mother, but was also afraid of experiencing it; that she hated her mother's trade; that she could not trust men because she had seen many of them disappear from her mother's company, and her father was never around; that she was attracted to me (almost thirty years her senior) because she imagined me to be like her father, and also because her mother had challenged her to take her lovers from her and she was now competing with my wife; that she wanted to give love to a baby, husband, or now me in order to overcome her fear of loving—which had resulted from her mother's rejection and the loss of her grandmother.

So far as I could judge, these insights were experienced by her emotionally, when she was in a receptive and contemplative mood, and were enlarged upon by her further considerations. All the characteristics of therapeutic insights proposed by various therapists seemed to be present; they probably contributed to a reduction of nightmares and made sense out of some of her turmoil. Yet the insights did not lead to a permanent change in her habits, as the developments of the subsequent three years showed. Her continued vacillations might be epitomized by the following exchange on one of her troubled days. She was pacing the floor restlessly, avoiding my promptings to consider what was bothering her.

"Where are you heading?"

"Straight to hell. At least a part of me wants it."

"What kind of person do you want to be?"

"Sometimes bad, sometimes good."

"And the hard thing about it is that the decision is in your

15

hands?" She nodded in acquiescence.

During the following few weeks she behaved in a subdued, controlled way both in interviews and in the institution. One day she sent an urgent note to me. "You have to see me." When she arrived, she said she had come to take leave. Some girls have prevailed on her to try to escape that night. "If you won't say anything, I'll tell you how we're going to do it."

I reacted with disapproval. "How long are you going to fool with your own life? When are you going to steer yourself by your brains instead of playing like a child? You're no longer a child. Why follow others blindly instead of taking care of your own future?"

She responded defiantly. "What is there in the future to look forward to?"

"We won't go over that nonsense again. But I'm going to alert your cottage to prevent you in this crazy playing against your interests." The escape attempt was thwarted. On a visit to the cottage a few days later I saw Sandra in the corridor. She thanked me for saving her from trouble and took my hand in a gesture of reconciliation. I maintained my stern role. "You can't go on through life blundering, pushed by that part of you that hates you."

Tears of gratitude appeared in her eyes, allowing her only to whisper, "I'll try." But within two weeks she had again assumed a devil-may-care attitude. She was spiteful with cottage counselors, and threatened to ask the Superintendent to send her to the City Jail because there she could at least smoke.

"You're running away from something again."

"It gets so dead when I'm good. It's boring. Then I start thinking of something. But I'm a far cry from what I was. I can't think of any new tricks, and it's not interesting to repeat the old ones."

"You're drifting again instead of using your mind."

"No, but I would like to win a point over them."

"You are still being childish. What points are you trying to win with me?"

"You're too smart for me. You read me."

I took this as an indication that she felt that my interpretations clicked with her own sense of her underlying feelings. She pointed to a book on the desk. *A Girl Grows Up*. "Can I borrow it?"

16

"I'm not sure you're really interested."

She laughed. "May be I'll surprise you one day. I might decide to grow up."

"When is that going to happen?"

"When I make up my mind about it. I can be good when I want to."

One day, after leaving at the end of interview, she returned to the office. I was writing notes on the hour I had just spent with her. She grabbed the paper, tried to read it, and would not return it. Remaining seated, I said, "If you do not leave it on my desk in the next ten seconds I shall cancel our appointment for next week."

Defiantly, she kept trying to decipher the notes.

"All right, then we'll meet in two weeks, if you still want to come."

She did come. She spoke of how good she had tried to be in her cottage because she wanted to be considered for parole. "What would you say about me to the Parole Board?" she asked me.

"That you are smart enough to make a success in life, but that you have not yet decided whether to act the age of twelve or your own age of seventeen."

She smiled confidently.

The neurotic aspects of her personality became more apparent. I was pleased because I imagined that therapy was progressing satisfactorily, for I had assumed the validity of the psychoanalytic view that a character disorder has to be led through neurotic phases toward normalcy. Margaret E. Fries (1949) quotes Eichhorn about treatment of behavior problems and delinquency: "There is no method of direct treatment for this type of disorder. If treatment is successful in making it impossible for the child to express his inner conflict in this form, he will then have to resort to expressing it in a neurosis. The resulting neurosis can then be treated by psychoanalysis, and in this way the problem of treating wayward children is solved."

One day as she sat in the office she became tense, her eyes fixed to the bottom of the book cabinet. "Is that a mouse?" she asked, trembling. I looked and discerned a ball of threads and dust, picked it up, and brought it to the desk.

Sandra moved her chair away from the desk. "I used to play

17

with mice when I was younger," she mused aloud, "even picked up a garden snake and put it around my arm when I was in the Junior High. But now mice and snakes bother me so much in my dreams that I wake up shaking."

"You're trembling even now. You'll be a nervous wreck if you continue the way you've been handling yourself in the last few years. You are destroying your good senses by letting yourself drift into foolishness. I see that you feel pretty miserable. If you want to work more earnestly to change yourself, I can see you again twice a week for a period of time."

She thanked me, said she would try, but there was no conviction in her tone.

In the next interview I had a chance to see how strongly embedded this neurotic reaction was in her. I tried a crude deconditioning experiment with her. I made a rough drawing of a mouse on a piece of paper, held it on my palm, then asked Sandra to stretch out her arm so I could transfer the drawing to her hand. She half-stretched her arm, then jumped up from her chair, stared fearfully at the drawing, and finally screamed "Take it away!" At other times she would jump if a fly crawled toward her, or a spider passed by on the floor.

I asked her, "Are you, perhaps, overdoing your show of nervousness so that I won't dare stop you?"

She reacted with an angry gesture, then smiled. "You guessed it right again."

"Who in your family is as jittery as you are, Sandra?"

"My grandpa is. He can't sit still. Mother isn't, though she has ulcers which may not be any better. I'm mostly like my uncle Billy. He doesn't feel like working. He has a wife who is seven years older. She works steady for the family, and he only off and on. But he does worse things than I do, in a bigger way."

"Do you want to be like them?"

"No. They're fools."

"Can you think of some woman you knew and respected that you want to be like?"

She was silent for quite a while, then said slowly; "I never knew any woman that I admired. But I might like to be a psychologist or something like that one day." Apparently she wanted to identify with my role with her.

I felt discouraged with this great void of female identification

18

figures in Sandra. Other girls, less disturbed than Sandra, identified with some members of the institutional staff, female student visitors, or other women in the community.

One day, after several interviews of evasive behavior, she revealed the dilemma that kept her in suspense and fed her turmoil. She stormed into the office agitated and angry; asked irrelevant questions; chatted; and disregarded my suggestions that she was trying to look away from something. Finally she said that she had quarreled with a friend and called her a little whore, and the other had retorted with "professional prostitute."

"This hurts you deeply?"

"The truth hurts. She knows what we were doing together. Often we'd see who could take more men. The most I took was seven. I couldn't look at them any more. . . . It's awful. When I think now of leaving this place, that's what I'm afraid of. I wouldn't steal. But whenever I wanted to get something like a ball dress, or other things I'd get me a man. Last time we earned a lot of money and started talking about what to do with that money. Buy drinks? Go somewhere? Then I rented an apartment, and paid for eight months in advance. My fiance Max was my protector. He got some false identification papers for me, beat up a guy who wouldn't pay. . . .

"I started with it a little three years ago. After a year I was going quite strong. I was afraid of sickness, was taking douches often. Even now I bathe often. When I leave here, I might go to New York or Los Angeles to join a gang. That scares me."

"Do you understand now why you are so tense and unhappy? You're gambling with your life. Can you expect to have any inner peace until you decide to turn away from the life you despise even when you lord it over men and get money from them?"

She nodded sadly and continued. "I hate paid sex. It was the first time in California, after grandma died. I must have gotten drunk before that soldier took me. I often feel pain in the abdomen after it."

"So you are violating your feelings by going into prostitution. Isn't that harder on you than to decide to earn your living by some hard work?"

"Yes, I want to break away from it. That's why I was thinking of taking you up on the training in commercial art. You mentioned that I could take it through the Rehabilitation Division.

19

Now I want to see the counselor you told me about."

When the Superintendent told her that in a month she would be going home in order to start the art school, Sandra became agitated again. She confided that two of her friends on parole—one a drunkard, the other a prostitute—had sent her a message that they would like her to join them.

"You are still undecided about what kind of woman you want to be. You aren't directing yourself, but letting the old habits carry you downstream," I remarked sadly.

She tried cynicism again. "It's more comfortable that way. Why struggle?"

"You are blinding yourself again. You know that you will be punished by unhappiness. that you'll feel like a wreck if you return to the old ways. Actually you'll have more pain in the long run if you don't struggle." She remained slumped in her chair. Feeling angry and disappointed, I asked; "Were all the hours a waste?"

"No. Really. Oh, you don't think I'm paying attention to what you're saying, but I am. At night I often think of what we said. And I am not in trouble so often. Sometimes I hear your voice when I do something wrong, but it's usually too late."

"Haven't you been doing the same to yourself? You shut off your conscience when you start rushing into something wrong instead of paying attention to it before you take the wrong step, then your conscience makes you feel bad—just as you expect me to be angry with you for going against your best interests."

"Oh, I'll be good. I've decided on that."

I shrugged my shoulders, deliberately showing disbelief, in order to challenge her.

Once, on parole, Sandra escaped from the workhome and disappeared from the supervision of the parole agent. Four months later a male voice asked for me on the telephone. "Sandra wants to talk to you."

Her voice was hoarse, her words blurred. I asked; "Are you now using dope too?"

There was some noise of male and female voices in the background. Sandra screamed at them to be quiet. Apparently she was the boss, for the noise ceased. "They're going to ruin my living room," she remarked proudly.

I answered bluntly. "Not only the room but your life too. Are you back in the trade?"

She avoided answering, talking instead about how she had hurt her hip falling one day when she was drunk. I treated her rudely, partly deliberately, partly because my professional pride was crushed. "You sound drunk now too. If you want to go on destroying yourself by jumping into treacherous waters, don't ask me to push you off the boat."

"I'm sick. Can't hold down any food for weeks now."

"And you asked for the fourth cigarette in these fifteen minutes! If you want to pull yourself out of that mess, give yourself up and come back to this school."

"I'll kill myself before I do that. I have a bottle full of sleeping pills. I'm so nervous."

"And you'll stay that way until you stop doing what's wrong in your own judgment."

"Can't I see you and talk with you? I still love you."

"Yes, if you come back to the school and want to start helping yourself. You have to start thinking of what you can do with your life instead of how you can ruin it."

"I won't come to school." She was not aware that the school staff did not really care to have her back either.

Two months later, Sandra was brought to the institution from jail. A customer had accused her of infecting him with a venereal disease. She had also been involved in an auto accident. Her fiance was suspected of dope-peddling. She was emaciated and tremulous and cried profusely during the interview. "I know what's the matter with me," she sobbed out. "I've tried to live life too fast. What I should've done when sixteen, I did when I was twelve. Wild parties, drink, staying out all night. Now when seventeen I am doing what I might have done at twenty-one. I was always rushing."

"From what?"

"From myself, I guess."

"Did you try to forget in that way what you did not like about yourself?"

"Yes. My mother wouldn't let me live with her when I ran away from that workhome. My aunt wouldn't give me another chance either. I wanted to spite them—show they couldn't stop me."

21

"Like cutting off your nose to spite your face?"

She laughed. "You put it well."

Ten days later she felt sure that something was changed in my office but did not know what. "Nothing is changed in the office, Sandra, I wonder if something hasn't changed in you."

"Yes, I feel better than before. I'm happy and relaxed. I've decided to join them if I can't fight them. I can't fight you grown-ups."

"You don't think we care for you."

"Yes, I know you do. But I still don't want to take life seriously." She became playful, moved about the room nervously, touched me on one occasion as if inadvertently. I repeated the rule known to her, that she must not touch my body. She refrained from doing it again.

She reported in other interviews that she was holding her temper with a rather demanding cottage counselor. I harped on the old theme, "A more important thing is how you control your feelings when you leave the institution."

This angered her. "You're never satisfied. I've been good here, and that's enough. I want to hit you sometimes."

"It's good that you bring out what you feel, then we can decide which feelings we want to follow and which ones we have to keep down."

"Oh, you!" She protested against my trying to be an educator consistently. Maybe she was also protesting against my gradual abandonment of the old system of searching for past traumas and insights for antecedents to her behavior. She now had few opportunities to enjoy her misery by contemplating it; I was trying to hold her to the task of learning how to live sensibly.

On one occasion her teacher sent Sandra to see me because she refused to do a test. The fear of tests was part of her neurotic repertoire. On the Rorschach, which I had given her a few months before, she produced only eight responses, far too few for her average intellectual level and emotional liveliness. Her self-respect and confidence were seriously undermined by what she held against herself. By means of severe repression, she was struggling to maintain a precarious inner balance. She explained her reaction to the test: "I know it, I did study, but my mind just went blank." When I tried to lead her to consider the sources of her fears, she repeatedly changed the topic. She laughed: "Like you

22

told me about that deaf man who switched off his hearing aid when he didn't want to hear something." She certainly was not in the dark regarding some of the struggle within her.

She wondered what she would do when she left the school in a few months—Max had been good to her, stuck by her when she was in jail last time, and had even started working steady because she demanded it. But he drank and was moody. He wanted her to marry him. Ben, another man who liked her was more stable, didn't drink, and was away in the Army, but she had his address. I interpreted: "You want a stable marriage and you sense that Max is unreliable." She had apparently not gone that far in her daydreams, and refused to consider it.

The institution was no longer helpful to Sandra. She had spent more than two years in it, knew all the tricks of avoiding controls, and was learning only how to be more underhanded. On my suggestion, the parole agent sent Sandra to a workhome. When I told her of the opportunity, she because so excited that she left the office to take a drink of water—to still her "butterflies." Next morning she called me. She was overjoyed with how good "that lady" was to her. In the afternoon she called again. "I'm going to goof again. I'm so lonely, I can't stand it. I can't concentrate on crocheting or sewing. The lady gave me lots of pretty material, but I can't settle on anything." She did not want to take up the course in art about which she had been so enthusiastic before. Now she only wanted to die, to have everything over. I spoke to her longer than half an hour, trying to help her stem these regressive trends. She felt better, she said. She called often in the following two weeks, as she struggled to stay away from the old life of irresponsibility. Finally she ran away from the home.

A month later she telephoned to ask what I thought about her marrying Max. I reminded her of her doubts about the lack of responsibility she had noticed in Max. She was not sure about it now. "Anyway, I'm pregnant by him."

I did not change my view of this mismatching. "I still think you had better not marry someone with whom you may expect trouble."

A few weeks later she told me how delighted she was with her marriage to Max. He was working steady, they loved each other, and were looking forward to their baby, and she had gone to church several times and felt good about being among decent

23

people, although she could not get Max to go with her.

In the meantime, I had left the institution to work for a military clinic. Sandra could not quite accept the fact that I could not talk to her on the telephone as long as I had before, and could not see her in regular interviews. Once she came to show me her son, a healthy, handsome baby.

In the course of the following two years her communications became progressively less happy. She had fights with Max. He had gone back to spending most of his time with the old gang, drinking, pushing dope. I could give her only scant help. On one occasion she spent three hours in the waiting room to talk with me for fifteen minutes at the end of my usual working day. Apparently she was using this contact as an anchor in her worsening personal state and family situation.

She went back to drinking and wild parties for a while. Max threatened to kill her. She moved to her aunt's, carrying on her trade on the side. The aunt wanted to adopt the baby, but Sandra adamantly refused. The aunt told me that Sandra only occasionally played with her son, and completely neglected his feeding and washing. She left these responsibilities to her aunt. I again tried to help with insights, pointing out to Sandra that she was following in her mother's footsteps. She neglected the care of the baby, caroused as if she had no obligation to the child and to herself as a mother; and sought pleasures for herself. She left jobs she had begun in a laundry and later in an office, both after only a few days.

Sandra accepted these interpretations with temporary remorse that brought little change to her behavior. One day the aunt called me in panic. Sandra was impossible, quarrelsome, spending nights away from home, drinking, keeping bad company, bringing the fellows in sometimes. When I contacted Sandra, she talked about suicide. She was desperate because Max, though in jail, threatened revenge through his friends. Ben had asked her to come to him, but she was afraid to bring trouble upon him.

She agreed to my suggestion to seek help in the local mental hospital. I made the necessary contacts, but she never went to the hospital. Since I have had no further contacts with Sandra I assumed that she must have gone to Ben in an attempt to control her childish pattern through the support of a more responsible man.

24

It might be remarked that Sandra was a massively disturbed individual; that one could have predicted that her psychotherapy would not be successful; and her responses proved nothing about the ineffectiveness of using insight in psychotherapy of delinquents. Such remarks may have some validity. On the other hand the question can be posed: If professionally trained psychotherapists cannot help in severely maladjusted cases, of what use are they in work with delinquents? If psychotherapists cannot bring about better social patterns in entrenched delinquents, shouldn't they leave the field to traditional correctional staffs who fail with hard cases and succeed with easier ones?

Their failures with difficult cases lead some therapists to seek alibis. They propose that the selection of cases for treatment should be more careful, knowledgeable, and precise. Yet the prognostic instruments are poor, based either on the subjective intuitive reaction of the interviewer, or on insufficiently validated empirical criteria or psychological tests. Lacking any unquestionably valid prognostic instruments, I had fixed upon the patient's decision as the best guide for taking anyone into psychotherapy. So long as patients kept their appointments and showed willingness to struggle with themselves the hours were, in some way, meaningful to them even if they did not develop at rates dictated by the therapist's ambitions and pressures for time.

In this way, Sandra was a good subject. She took the initiative for therapy; the therapist rarely sought her. In fact I often indirectly rejected her by being demanding and unsympathetic toward her immature behavior. She kept coming back, presumably because therapy provided something valuable for her, although this did not coincide with my own goals. Her progress was halting and transient although, in several ways, she gave the impression that she was inwardly stirred.

Sandra's ineffective response to insight in psychotherapy was far from isolated. The purpose of this introduction excludes a more exhaustive documentation. But my notes contain examples of other delinquent girls who were unable or, to put it more correctly, unwilling to use insights from therapy to change their established, maladapted behavioral patterns. Like Sandra, they had a warm friendly feeling for the therapist. They remained in trusting contact with me after they left the institution, but did not

25

seem to care for attaining a deeper and comprehensive view of themselves as persons.

Perhaps they lack the compulsion some educated people have to achieve a logical view of themselves. They have lived primarily by impulse rather than by thought and are somewhat resistant to any attempt to lead them to a better-organized, more sensible comprehension of their existence. This may be disappointing to therapists with middle-class notions. Apparently these nonintellectualizing delinquents cannot utilize the sort of therapy misused by some well-to-do ladies who can stand thousands of hours of so-called "analysis," enjoying it as a mild stimulus alongside drinks, coffee, bridge parties, and gossip. The delinquents are more action-minded. That might be one of the reasons why Sandra and other girls achieved, at least temporarily, a stabler reaction pattern after I took action or pressured them instead of handling them in permissive, neutral, nondirective fashion.

Insight Demoted

It is of interest to consider in this connection the method of treating delinquents devised by the best known psychoanalytic therapist in this field, August Eichhorn (1955). Freud wrote the forword to his book, *Wayward Youth,* and Eissler (1949) edited a volume of essays dedicated to Eichhorn's seventieth birthday leaving no doubt as to the revered place Eichhorn occupied in psychoanalytic circles. Yet the methods of giving psychological help to delinquents, as described in *Wayward Youth,* show a minimal use of verbally communicated insights in contacts with delinquents. "The treatment of delinquents is a matter of re-education," writes Eichhorn. He denies that he was conducting psychoanalysis in his eminently successful work with dissocial personalities. What he did was close to the methods a psychoanalytically trained social worker would use with delinquents nowadays.

Eichhorn's success appears to have come from his exceptionally patient handling of delinquents and from his unshakable belief in human beings. He was tireless in his efforts on their behalf, and won them over by his warm humanity and sure handling. He acted more like a wise and shrewd educator than an analyst.

Although he used the psychoanalytic theory of personality in achieving brilliant understanding of the emotional dynamics of his charges, he does not report any consistent use of his insights in helping delinquents achieve a personal comprehension of their misbehaviors. He did not reveal to them the unconscious promptings which he thought he clearly discerned in their aggressive and immature attitude. They grew out of their dissocial behavior in the same natural unconscious way they had grown into them under the unwholesome influences of their families and environment.

My experiences with delinquents, without embracing psychoanalytic theories in a serious way, suggest that Eichhorn would have been just as successful in his redemptive work if he had viewed delinquents through some other system, e.g. Adler's.

Pfister (1949), writing in the commemorative volume, explains Eichhorn's remarkable success by the love he actively used in his work with delinquents. It was a love expressed as warm respect, forgiveness, forebearance, and self-denial. Pfister points out that many educators had been able to straighten out the distorted lives of delinquents prior to the advent of psychoanalysis. Thinking further along this line, we might note that dedicated Roman Catholic priests and nuns who, though unacquainted with Freudian thought, had given stability to thousands of potential offenders. At the opposite ideological extreme, Soviet educators, rejecting psychoanalysis as a bourgeois perversion, report their success with delinquents.

As an illustration of their efforts a film widely shown in Europe before World War II, entitled *The Road Into Life,* deals with the rehabilitation of some vicious Russian delinquents, the *"bezprizorni."* Its thesis, of course, was that such prodigious tasks can be carried out only by humanitarians inspired by Marxist doctrines. What was obvious from the movie was that the leader's attitude of respect and trust toward his charges awakened and sustained in them a feeling of self-respect that led to an awareness of conscience and more acceptable social behavior.

The considerate attitude shown by various counselors, irrespective of the particular ideology to which they subscribed, may well have been the primary curative factor. Just so, a basic respect for the human being in trouble might well be a principal therapeutic influence, regardless of the special techinque favored by

27

a particular therapist. Thus it is the love in action that helps the delinquent and probably many other patients.

Seguin (1965) proposes the concept of "psychotherapeutic eros." Dr. Fries (1949) expresses a similar conclusion: "The child stops his asocial behavior not out of insight derived from analytic procedure, because that would take too long, but out of love toward the analyst to whom he has developed this extremely strong transference and whom he would not wish to disappoint."

Uniqueness of Every Psychotherapy

In trying to formulate general principles for psychotherapeutic treatment one sometimes loses sight of the other side of the picture. Generalizations tend to obscure the unique features of every psychological therapy. Every treatment is different from every other because it is influenced by the interactions of three highly individualized conditions:

1. The patient with his multitude of needs, emotions, values, and potentialities, both conscious and unconscious, expressed directly or deviously.

2. The therapist with his multitude of feelings, fluctuating motivations, moral values, and theoretical bias and blindspots, both conscious and unconscious, expressed directly or deviously.

3. The environment, with its rewards and punishments, permissions and prohibitions, inconsistencies and insensitive pressures, stated clearly or implied, enforced sternly or haltingly.

The great variety of elements which enter into psychotherapy is bound to produce unique patterns in the emotional states of the patient. Since these contributing forces change from one moment to another, causing constant shifts, there is no way of fully describing, in a static fashion, any psychotherapeutic situation. At best one can describe the main features of the patient, therapist, environment, and some of their interactions, leaving the build-up of the composite picture to the reader's imagination. The patients are described and the method exemplified in Part I. The therapist, his method, and the immediate environment, i.e. the correctional institution, is described as follows:

The days when the therapist was considered an impersonal sounding board for the patients' associations have become part of the distant past for the greater number of contemporary psychologists. Even in those early days, the supposedly detached therapist influenced a patient by many of his personal values and attitudes. By way of example, open and subtle influences upon the patient differed drastically in the practices of Freud, Stekel, and Jung, even before the apostasy of the two disciples, because each started with different views of the human being with whom he was to develop one of the most intimate of psychological contacts.

Freud was wary of close human contacts and kept the therapy relationship at an impersonal level; he was also consciously and unconsciously bent upon alienating clients from the prevalent Roman Catholic culture which had caused him a great deal of pain and injustice through its anti-Semitism.

Stekel interacted more directly with his clients, and was more attuned to the dictates of their conscience as an important personality force, one which should not be violated or disregarded. Freud's theoretical view was, on the contrary, that patients should be liberated from the tyranny of the superego which supposedly contributed to their neurotic turmoil.

Jung, with his philosophical and religious background, was bound to lead his patients toward the solutions of emotional and existential problems different from those sought by the atheist Freud or the pragmatically-oriented Stekel.

The role of the therapist's person had been often stressed. Even in psychoanalysis, which traditionally has emphasized the technical aspects and neutrality, there is a growing recognition of the importance of the therapist's personality on the course of analysis. Nacht (1962) writes: ". . . the person of the analyst . . . is a decisive factor, and that is why I have often maintained that it is what the analyst *is* rather then what he *says* that matters." He points out that the fundamental weapon of psychoanalysis, interpretation, is ineffective if there is no satisfying human relationship between the analyst and his subject. Nacht stresses that a relationship of love rather than of neutrality is particularly essential for psychotherapeutic work with patients who had suffered *actual* trauma: "It is only when these patients unconsciously perceive, or are obscurely aware of this open and attentive attitude, this genuinely compassionate acceptance, that they have at last the certainty of being understood and accepted with their yearnings. Their emotional climate is in this way changed and they can at last make their peace, first with themselves and then with the world—in a word, they in turn can love."

The life histories of most girls described in Part I contain many actual traumas and obviously fall within the category requiring "compassionate acceptance." When I reflect on the psychotherapy I conducted with these delinquent girls, I can clearly discern that much of what I did was determined by the type of person I was, by the experiences which shaped my own psychological course, and by the moral, religious, social, and cultural views I held.

With the surety of actual experience I approached the problems of these disturbed adolescents in the way I had struggled with my own postadolescent crises. I had resolved the turmoil of early manhood by adopting service to others as the means of liberating myself from dependent reactions, mild depressions, and threatening disorientation. I had found, in traditional Christianity and in time-tested general moral precepts, the inexhaustible sources of psychological self-healing.

When the girls were troubled with sexual urges, aggressive feelings, uncertainties, and restlessness, I had no doubt as to where the solution lay: in subjecting their biological drives to social demands, and in bypassing transient impulsive pleasures in preference to obedience to moral and spiritual principles. After all, some of the finest human beings in history have achieved a firm emotional balance, and even greatness through the conviction that the raw forces of human nature, the passions, have to be enobled by reason, virtue, self-denial, spirituality, devotion to God, or some other humanizing principle.

Influenced by what I had learned from my own development, I conceived the psychopathology with which I struggled in my patients as arising mainly from unsettled moral problems, from failure to control hostility, sexual drives, socially irresponsible behavior, and self-centeredness. There were, of course, traumatic or other antecedents or "explanations" for irresponsible actions,

30

and I often saw these girls as victims of parental psychopathology; yet their personal histories did not absolve them from acting less responsibly than any other member of society.

Thus I did not dwell exhaustively on their past traumas, although I found it psychotherapeutically useful to give the girls an opportunity to ventilate their griefs and frustrations, and the sharing of sorrows established a warm and friendly atmosphere for our relationship. Yet the dominant direction of my effort was away from lamentation over injustices and handicaps, and toward a consideration of what they might do to avoid such troubles in the future. I asked them what kind of person they wanted to be in ten or fifteen years; what kind of adult they admired, and if they wanted to pay the price of punishment or unhappiness by indulging in an irresponsible course of action dictated by impulse.

I often considered with them in detail the steps they would have to follow to arrive at the goals which they set, the pitfalls in themselves, and in their environment they would have to guard against, and the steps they would need to take when discouragement threatened.

When the girls were bewildered, guilty, dismayed, or depressed I would not let them enjoy their misery too long. In various ways I asked them, "Where do you go now? How do you want to work on this? How do you get out of this unpleasant inner state? How can you live with this irritation?" The question was less often "Why did this befall you? How did this unhappy condition come about?" and more often "How and where do you choose to go from here?" It was not "Why?" but "Whither?" I took this orientation not only because it had been a part of my practical philosophy during the mature part of my life, but also because I was influenced by Adler's *Individual Psychology,* by G. Allport's (1955) *Becoming,* and also by some existentialist writings. Adler emphasizes one's goals in life as determining psychopathological developments and recovery from them. Allport points to the future-oriented intentional dispositions as the foundation for personality growth. He remarks, humorously, that although normal people look forward, the psychologists were misled to look backward. The existentialists emphasize the future as the most important aspect of man's relationship to time.

I neither preached nor moralized; the precepts of both nondirective and psychoanalytic therapies wisely warn against this.

31

However, I did not hesitate to offer my mature ego and superego as a guide to the immature egos of these girls. They used this support as a crutch until they became sufficiently strong to control their impulses by rational, moral, and long-term considerations. Dr. William Glasser (1961, p. 50) writes about the benefits derived from "borrowed ego" strength. He postulates a basic psychological principle: "To develop an effective ego, a person must have a meaningful two-way relationship with someone who has an effective ego—a relationship in which the ego of the giving person is available for use by the receiving person in a consistent atmosphere of some love and a minimum of hostility and anger." I feel that the relationships described in the forthcoming pages approximate this principle.

I served in various roles, as required by individual girls at various stages of development: substitute parent, confidant, confessor, repressor, counselor, protector from the danger of impulses, moral guide, inspirer, trusted friend, respecter of their persons, critic of their foolishness. The title of this book, *No Water in My Cup,* taken from Dora's poem, symbolically expresses the therapeutic role I wished to perform: filling the cup of the psyche—depleted through the girl's own mistakes and the depravity of others—with fresh contents of hope, self-respect, peace of mind, mastery over disintegrative trends, social responsibility, a sense of well-being, of living under conscience, of conquering the existential void, and of living a fuller and freer life. Other and more technical details about the method employed are given in Part II.

I do not feel I employed a distinctive method with my subjects, or claim universal applicability to my approach. I have tried the method with other types of patients, both at an outpatient military clinic and in private practice, and it has worked satisfactorily for me and my patients. Other therapists may find it less appropriate to their strengths and weaknesses and may reject it as ineffective for them. The method might be considered more akin to behavioral approaches to psychotherapy than to those relying chiefly on insight; it has some affinities to existential therapy and moral retraining. If a name need be given, I would suggest the title of the *psychosynth-ethic* method, for the attainment of ethically responsible behavior is viewed as the main curative and integrative agent against emotional disturbances.

32

As the environment in which the girls spent most of their hours, in contrast with one or two hours they had with the therapist weekly, the institution performed an essential role in the behavioral reactions which the subjects showed in the interview situation.

The institution was relatively small, with about 120 girls. They lived in cottages, eighteen to thirty of them in each building; attended a high school on the grounds; and their average stay in the institution was twelve to fifteen months.

The regimen in the institution was quite strict. Full obedience to cottage counselors was required and enforced by withdrawal of such privileges as talking at the table, recreation, home visits, and so on. More serious breaches of discipline were punished by confining a girl to her room, postponement of parole, appearance before the superintendent and other threats. The pressure toward obedience and respect for rules was constant, but there were no loud reproaches or physical maltreatment.

The overall purpose of the training was to compel the rebellious adolescents to consider more seriously the demands of authority and society when planning a course of action. Many of them became better adjusted to societal demands by gaining a sharpened awareness of the self-interest involved in accepting social limitations. Many of them experienced security and gratification of their dependent needs for the first time in their lives by being exposed to the consistently firm adults. Their frustration tolerance was increased and temptations toward impulsive acting-out reduced. Repression of impulsive behavior seemed to be one of the major achievements of institutional training.

Suppression of impulses for fear of punishment may not be considered a healthy operation by some professional workers. Although not the ideal method for reeducation, under the training circumstances, this suppression did lead to the desired result of better interpersonal and intrapersonal adjustment for the larger part of these delinquents. Since their maladjustment consisted of a disregard for social rules, they could be considered improved if they gave up the irresponsible behavior that ignored both the interests of others and their own long-term needs. An essentially similar

33

view is expressed by a psychoanalytically-oriented writer, Lippman (1949, p. 164): "At the present time our institutions for delinquent children are used as a last resort in a treatment program, when all measures for direct psychiatric treatment and environmental manipulation fail. Ideally the institutions should be used early, particularly for treatment of many of the chronic young delinquents who would welcome an opportunity to live in an impersonal setting in which they are not expected to develop an emotional tie to parents, and where therapy with them could be carried on. It would be well, also, to use the institutions early for many of the aggressive delinquent youngsters who for a number of reasons have failed to control their instinctual drives. They are uninhibited, defiant, and contemptuous of any casework methods. Before their aggression and attitudes are modified, it is unavailing to place them in foster homes because few, if any, foster parents are able to deal with the punishing behavior of these aggressives. Supervised treatment for a year or more in an institution may be sufficient to help others, and to live socially in a community. Their problem is much more one of control and restraint, than a resolution of inner conflict."

The foregoing considerations are an important component of the overall effects of psychotherapy in the institution. I generally approved of the main trends of the institutional pressures toward a more socialized and conforming personality orientation. I did not agree with some excessively punitive and rigid demands on the part of some cottage counselors, but I always encouraged the girls to comply with the requirements of "the powers that be" as a realistic acceptance of those irritations which we cannot avoid in many group situations.

I structured my interpretations to the girls so that they might realize they were being challenged now—as they would be in later life—to live under unpleasant circumstances without creating further aggravations through thoughtless reactions. In terms of transference feelings, I might have appeared to the girls as a weak but comforting Daddy, while the consistently demanding cottage counselors were unconsciously identified as strict, often threatening Mammas.

The institutional pressures on the girls, and even the unconsciously sadistic behavior of one or two counselors was at no time detrimental to the course of therapy. In fact the intense hostility

34

and attendant anxiety aroused in the girls by conflicts with stern adults could be considered more as a contribution to the psychotherapeutic progress. The girls were driven by training pressures to openly abandon aggressive behavior and seek more constructive ways of coping with rage or frustration. They had to work more intensely in therapy to adopt mature and socially acceptable methods of handling hostility and irritations.

The useful fusion of institutional pressures and therapeutic process was primarily the result of the closed setting of the institution. The avenues for acting-out were well blocked, so that the girls were thrown upon the necessity of psychological manipulations. In an open setting these rigid and insistent demands would have led to hostile outbursts, but the institution represented an inexorable reality. "There are too many opportunities," as Lippman (1949) says, "for gratifying aggressive drives in the community, and those gratifications seem to lessen the wish to continue treatment."

Two Precursors

A year or two after I had finished compiling this study I became acquainted with the thinking and the psychotherapeutic practice of O. Hobart Mowrer and William Glasser, whose views are in certain essential ways akin to my own. They go much further in their revolutionary proposals for psychotherapy than I had at that time dared. If I had had the encouragement of these two seminal thinkers in liberating myself more completely from the prevailing Freudian concepts of psychotherapy, my psychotherapeutic approach might have been more decisive. The reported results might have been even more decisive, for I probably would have abandoned my attempt to achieve a compromise between the direct (behavioral) and the uncovering (analytic) methods of therapy used in this research.

Professor Mowrer (1961, 1964) reached his theoretical position partly through his own suffering and the failure of his psychoanalysis to provide healing from tormenting depressions. He had several hundred hours of psychoanalysis with three analysts over a period of thirteen years, but with no lasting relief. He was compelled by the impass in which he found himself to take a fresh look at his troubles.

He discovered by intuitive understanding and empirical trial that psychoanalysis had misled him about what really mattered within him as a person. He concluded that the Freudian advice of toning down the supposedly overstrict superego was an ill-given direction, exacerbating the neurotic conflict. He developed a psychotherapeutic approach—Integrity Therapy—of heeding the conscience and giving it primacy among the motivational promptings, thereby achieving personality integration.

The method concentrates on the violation of values held by patients themselves. The agrieved conscience is seen as the principal source of emotional disturbance. The alignment of behavior with professed moral values, restitution of some sort, and avoidance of duplicity are seen as the main curative agents.

Of course these principles are not new. They were known to sages and saints of older cultures. We, twentieth century barbarians, inheriting the spiritual confusion initiated by the thinkers of the so-called Enlightenment, have lost sight of the basic laws of the human psyche.

In asserting principles known clearly to cultures less traumatized by technical and rationalistic trends, Professor Mowrer seems to be undertaking a necessary service to both the emotionally disturbed and their would-be deliverers.

Others have abandoned the Freudian method for other reasons. It is of interest that another famous psychologist, Boring (1940), also found psychoanalysis useless in lifting his depression. Wortis (1954), a prominent psychiatrist, was so disappointed with the didactic analysis he undertook with Freud that he chose to give up the prospect of a lucrative practice rather than employ what appeared to him an unpromising way of healing the emotionally troubled. Ellis (1957) practiced psychoanalysis first, abandoned it for a psychoanalytically-oriented therapy, and finally developed his own system of Rational-Emotive Therapy. He finds results with patients much more reassuring with his new method.

It might well be that of the three principal functions of psychoanalysis—a theory of personality, a method for investigation of intricacies of human mind, and a system of psychotherapy—the last function may be abandoned as cumbersome, impractical, and inefficient in producing behavioral improvements. Patients, in order to recover emotional balance, may not need brilliant and

36

deep interpretations and insights. What appears valuable in building an impressive personality theory, or achieving the "discovery" of hidden motives, may easily be an unnecessary handicap to recovery from emotional disturbance.

A well-known psychoanalyst, Glover (1931), gave his colleagues a useful hint which however, was largely disregarded. Glover experimented with "inexact interpretations" and found them as useful to the patients as those which were theoretically correct. It seems that in spite of their emphasis upon the unconscious roots of behavior, psychoanalysts have often relied too heavily on rational structuring of their responses according to theoretical preconceptions. Like witchdoctors ascribing the recovery of patients to formulae and incantations, psychoanalysts and other psychotherapists attribute the recovery of their patients to the content of their interviews, although the recovery may in fact be better accounted for by some factors which remain obscured by theoretical biases.

Dr. William Glasser (1963) developed his Reality Therapy in a direction diametrically opposed to the prevalent "psychodynamic" and nondirective methods. Working with offenders and patients who had been hospitalized for years, he and another psychiatric colleague, Dr. G.A. Harrington, evolved since 1956 a system of psychotherapy closer to commonsense views of thinkers and educators of all civilized societies. The following excerpts are from a mimeographed copy of the address Dr. Glasser gave in 1963 at the Annual Governors Conference on Youth in Chicago:

Reality Therapy, as the name implies, deals with reality, present reality, and holds that what is more important is facing this reality responsibly. The future must be considered, but the patient's past, except as it is directly related to his present behavior, is of little importance. Discussing his history is in fact antitherapeutic because it serves to minimize the importance of present behavior. We also completely disregard any unconscious processes; we are not interested in looking for supposedly unconcious reasons for his difficulties.

We are only interested in present conscious behavior and whether he and we think he is acting in a responsible way and pointing toward a responsible future. As a part of our deep concern with his present behavior, we help him to acknowledge a set of values as early in the therapy as possible. We then discuss his behavior in terms of whether he thinks he is doing right or wrong according to these values. There is usually little difficulty in arriving at his values; the difficulty lies in helping him to live responsibly in accordance with them.

Much of the therapy time therefore centers on whether he is doing right or wrong according to his values.

....

We are not concerned with isolated feelings. If the patient is sad, depressed, angry, empty, fearful, or anxious, he must relate these feelings to what he is doing now and determine whether his behavior is responsible. No one can help a patient *feel better;* he can only be helped to *do* better, which means live a more responsible life. Never claiming that therapy can make anyone happy, we do not even concern ourselves with happiness, only with responsibility.

Our theory holds that the diagnosis of mental illness is artificial and meaningless because what we are really seeing is some manifestation of irresponsibility. All mental symptoms and disturbed behavior are the result of an inability to live a responsible life according to one's values.

....· ....

We certainly do not deny that a person's history has led to his present behavior. It is the present behavior, nevertheless, which we must treat; in fact it is all we can treat. *No one can treat a man's history.* Our experience has shown that a person's conscious acceptance of responsibility must be broadened, and that what is unconscious is of little importance because it merely accompanies the overt symptoms.

....

. . . the therapist must become deeply involved with the patient. Meeting the patient on as high a level as the patient can attain, he must never be aloof, sacrosanct, or superior. The psychiatrist must be responsible enough to bare his own values, his feelings, and some of his be-

38

havior in the conversation which makes up the therapy. The therapist must by example show the patient that acting responsibly has rewards. A therapist who is not a strong, responsible person can help no one.

....

Patients treated by Reality Therapy never sing the familiar refrain "I'm this way because of my mother." We feel that regardless of what the patient's mother was like the patient still is responsible for the way he is, and only he can change. Perhaps, if he changes his behavior, his mother may change hers; but whether she does or not, he must.

An essential technique, therefore, of Reality Therapy is never to ask "Why?" only "What?" to avoid any implication that the patient is not responsible for his behavior. We think the classical question of "Why?" has led psychiatry down a blind alley because it helps the patient to evade reality.

....

We know that therapy which advocates the uncovering of unconscious conflicts seems to work in many cases, especially with people who are not too disturbed and who are already moderately responsible. With mental hospital patients and severe behavior disorders, we have never seen it work. When traditional therapy does work, however, we believe it is because of the therapist's involvement and the kind of person he is, not the theory. We think that therapy needs to be directed to conscious responsibility, and that unconscious conflicts necessarily accompany disturbed behavior but they do not cause it.

It is obvious from the above excerpts that Professor Mowrer's and Dr. Glasser's views converge in several important ways: In giving primacy to values and superego; in concern with the present and future and not with the past; in challenging the patient to responsible behavior instead of concentrating on feelings as traditional therapy does; in seeing the source of psychopathology in the disregard of one's values and not in childhood traumas; in viewing psychopathology as irresponsibility rather than as "mental illness."

It is also apparent from the foregoing parts of the Introduction and from the forthcoming descriptions of the psychotherapy carried out with delinquent girls that I worked on similar assumptions, though without arriving at the theoretical decisiveness of my two precursors or achieving such a clean break with prevalent Freudian psychotherapeutic traditions as they.

PART I

WHAT WE SAID AND DID:

THE GIRLS AND THEIR REACTIONS IN PSYCHOTHERAPY

WHAT WE SAID AND DID:

THE GIRLS AND THEIR REACTIONS
IN PSYCHOTHERAPY

These brief summaries are offered as examples of personality backgrounds; the main problems dealt with in therapy; and the reaction of the girls to psychotherapeutic processes, particularly their relationship to the therapist. In chronological order the summaries roughly follow the events as they took place in therapy and primarily use the expressions of the girls themselves.

Ann

Age 14, IQ bright normal, 41 interviews in seven months. Committed for running away, stealing, promiscuity. Referred to me because she was not making any progress in institutional adjustment after six months. She was described by teachers and counselors as moody, listless, sneaky, spiteful.

She complained of sleeplessness and inability to concentrate. In the early interviews she wondered if she were going to "crack up" because she wanted to "make out" with a girl, and thinks of her often. She had so much fun with men outside. She was popular, though some jealous girls called her a slut; it hurt. She would try to stay at home for a month, then would get into "circulation" again. Soon she expressed dissatisfaction with me: She could have so much fun with me as a man; yet there I sit, torturing her with my solemnity and disinterest. While speaking of her sexual exploits, she concluded: "I'm dying of curiosity to see how you do it." The topic came up often during the first twenty meetings.

Slowly, she began to accept my repeated interpretations: That her desires were a repetition of earlier habits through which she tried to feel better by conquering men—as if to add them to her collection; that I could be of more value to her as a therapist by helping her achieve happiness within herself as a person, than as a man who could relieve her sexual frustrations; that babies cannot deny or postpone desires and grown-ups have to strive for responsibile behavior, as she will have to do in growing up; that we have to take into account our need for self-respect and the respect of others, our moral obligations and long-term goals instead of seeking satisfaction at the first sexual urge.

Once she reported that she "made out" with a girl but wondered why she had not enjoyed it as before. I pointed to the awakening of another part of her feelings—her conscience. Slowly she reported that she had rejected another girl's invitation to "go the rounds" (homoerotic friendship), and refused to exchange shoes with another girl. She said she was finding her work in the kitchen more interesting, that a counselor had praised her for the first time, and that she was no longer as quarrelsome with other girls as she had been. She was surprised to find she was no longer angry with her dad and mom. She had been thinking the other day that she would like to join one of the school clubs when she left the institution; she had scoffed at these clubs before as being only for "squares." She wondered how she could ever have enjoyed the company of fellows who went around in T-shirts and ragged levis, and who bragged about stealing or using dope and of not being able to hold any job.

"It's like I was really tired and couldn't see straight. Then I got to sleep and rested and could see clearly when I woke up. Now I'll be able to tell my old friends at home that I've got other things to do in life. Won't quarrel with them; just tell them that there are other pleasures I want to have now: go skating, have good grades, take an art course, maybe dancing lessons. Life can be interesting without the things I thought were fun before that just bring you trouble. I'm much happier now."

I reinforced these changes towards social conformity as signs of her maturing, of finding ways to have fun without subsequent regrets. There were ups and downs in her adjustment to work demands in the cottage and school, yet teachers and counselors were becoming more satisfied with her. She would become pouty, angry or jealous, but would give these reactions in interviews as childish. It had become a standard remark for me to quietly say "baby" when she regressed. She would smile and promise she would grow up one day. She later reported becoming annoyed

44

at the squabbling of other girls about trivia. "They're just like babies. You take their toy truck from them, and they cry as if there was nothing else left in the world."

She saw that her parents, who had separated then come to live together again, were childish in many ways. She became fearful that they would upset her by buying her things instead of trying to talk with her and understand her feelings. A recurring question that came up was: "Are they again going to give in to me when I get angry, or are they going to lay down the law to me as they should?"

She wished I could come with her to help her in those first months on parole. She was glad now that I had not given in to her desires in the beginning, so she could come to find a friend in me. She intended to call me long distance when she felt upset. I reassured her about her ability to resist temptations and solve problems in the family and at school.

To summarize, Ann grew rapidly from a spiteful, labile teenager, dominated by sexual and aggressive drives, into a young woman with appropriate ambitions and willingness to submit to societal demands and authority.

Six months after her departure from the institution, I had an opportunity to talk with the probation officer in her hometown. She was doing well at school and at home, and appeared happy and stable. At Christmastime she sent me a card thanking me for the help I had given her.

Test Changes

The scores on test scales are provided as objective descriptions of individual changes in the girls in therapy. These data are supplied as comparisons with the qualitative descriptions. Only the marked changes are highlighted in these numerical summaries. A change was considered marked if it was 10 or more points on MMPI clinical scales, 5 or more points on additional MMPI scales and on HGI-Ho scale; and 3 or more points on scales A to H of HGI and on 16 PF scales, as these are given in stens, ranging 1-10 score points. If the change can be interpreted as deterioration, the numbers are bracketed. The behavioral ratings on the Haggerty-Olson-Wickman Scales (HOW) are given for teachers (Tr) and for counselors (Cr) separately. The rating are cited fully even if the change was not large. The descriptions of scales are provided in Part II and in the Appendix.

MMPI: L (40-65), F 66-48, K 36-68, D 61-47, Pt 74-55, Sc 91-63, Ma 96-70, Si 63-37, At 38-5, A 36-4, Es 36-48, R (5-13), Dq 26-13, De 32-13, Do 8-17, Ca 21-7, Re 7-18, Ho 49-7, Ad 17-30, Dn 5-20, So-r (14-38).
16 PF: A 3-9, C 3-7, E (10-6), F 6-9, G 1-8, H 2-10, L 9-5, O 4-9, Q3 2-9, Q4 8-2.
HGI: Ho 51-16, A 7-3, B 9-4, C 10-1, D 5-1, E 7-0, F 4-1, G 9-6, H 5-2.
HOW: Tr 80-59, Cr 91-67.5.

Ann showed considerable personality changes on objective tests. There was a remarkable reduction in anxiety and hostility. Her excitability and inappropriate response to environmental stimuli was brought within normal limits. Her dependent needs were largely relinquished. She became capable of more mature and responsible behavior, as the ratings by teachers and counselors confirm. The delinquent trends were lessened. She was more outgoing instead of being wrapped up in her frustrations, and became less suspicious and tense. There was a considerable increase in her capacity to persist with enthusiasm toward chosen goals. Her guilt feelings became less troublesome to her, and she was eager to achieve social approval, which may account partially for her improved scores. On the whole, her defensiveness may be considered more as a sign of ego strength than of "halo-effect" or self-deluding trend.

Betty

Age 17, IQ normal, 21 interviews in three and one half months. Stocky, with fiery dark eyes and darting gestures. She was committed for uncooperativeness at home and school. The police alleged sexual activities with two older men, but she never admitted such behavior to me. I refrained from probing into this sensitive area.

Betty was referred to me because she seemed unrepentant after being confined to her room for three weeks for writing a passionate, obscene letter to another girl.

46

Betty complained, of her twin troubles—temper and worry. She was easily worried, and then her anger would be more quickly triggered. Anything could make her mad, particularly if a girl said "s.o.b." even if the comment was not directed at her.

Betty felt very bad about hurting the feelings of her mother, who suffered because Betty consistently provoked her stepfather's easily-aroused temper. Betty hated him because she imagined her real dad would have been much more loving; but she had never seen her real dad, who had separated from her mother when Betty was still a baby. She had lived with grandparents for a number of years, but found her grandmother oppressively strict. She liked her grandpa because he played games with her and she could tell him her problems.

It hurt her deeply when her grandparents finally separated after many loud quarrels in her presence. Sometimes she had joined in, the trio trying to outyell one another. In school she had fought teachers, boys, and girls. "I always felt I had to fight them because it seemed they wanted to defeat me."

She denied writing the obscene note, and spoke with apparent disgust about "making out" with that girl. The incident had happened unexpectedly when they met in the lavatory. During the following week Betty had felt sick to her stomach about it. "What would my mother say? How could my boy friend forgive me for it?"

I turned her attention to the uselessness of her self-aversion, and pointed out that she might help herself more by deciding to avoid intimacy with any tempting girl and by proving that this had been only a slip on her part. My intention was to lead her toward a nonneurotic handling of guilt. She gratefully grasped at the idea. Next time she reported that she had apologized to the counselors whom she had previously scorned. She felt that this was quite an achievement for her because she had never before admitted her faults. She was bothered when her friend still wore a medal she had given her. "I wouldn't mind if she kept it for what it is meant to be—saintliness. But she's still staring at me. It makes me sick."

Betty was startled by my suggestion that she and the other girl meet in my office so that we three could talk it over together. In the following interview she asked for such a meeting, and I called the other girl immediately. Betty spoke of the need for both of them to avoid the upsetting homosexual experiences. The

47

other girl, who had been sexually promiscuous since the age of five, did not seem impressed and on leaving she only promised coldly that she would think about it.

Betty was on the verge of despair for the remainder of our interview. I reinforced her self-esteem by pointing out that she had done the right thing, and that what others did was not important. After bolstering her self-respect, I proceeded to arm her with preventive self-knowledge. Part of her despair, I told her, was caused by the knowledge that she would have to fight her battle alone, betrayed by her partner's entrenchment in the offense which still remained attractive to her too.

Several interviews later Betty spoke of pleasant times she had had when she had been friends with the other girl before the breakthrough of homosexual activity. "Why does it come to my mind?"

I repeated my explanation: She wants love. It is harder to control "queer" urges when a breach is made even once in the defenses against them. All of us have many unacceptable desires and have to hold them in check. She responded: "That makes a lot of sense to me. I can handle it that way."

She turned her feelings toward her boy friend. For two or three weeks she considered her desire for him. She was fearful that either her parents or the parole authorities would prevent their marriage, although she was prepared to fight their interference. I encouraged her to take into account her own needs for further education as well as for avoiding past troubles. This probably helped her achieve some autonomy from sexual urges.

Soon, she saw that she ought to wait to see whether she and her boy friend might not have changed in their feelings toward each other. She now wanted to finish school and have some job experience before marriage. I supplied her with addresses of some correspondence schools. She wrote to them, and spent her free time studying. I reinforced this trend by pointing to her ability to sublimate her formerly tyrannical urges to sex or hostility.

All this time we waged an ongoing battle against her hostility. Some adult who she thought had deliberately provoked her was usually the focus of her rage. I challenged her impressions indirectly by asking how other girls felt about that person, and why. She realized, possibly for the first time in life, that she did not need to react with hostility to implied criticism.

She became open to the possibility that her perceptions might be mistaken without being threatened by the idea. After one or two interviews she reported that one of the counselors no longer seemed to be so ugly in appearance. "It's funny that I now seem to like T. though I hated her last week."

She was confined to her room for a week for being spiteful to another counselor, but later reported that she couldn't get over how nice Mrs. N. was being to her. She eargerly confirmed my hunch that these people were "nicer" because *she* was not provoking them any more. "It's me. I've been causing my own troubles," she would say smiling.

When sent to work in the administration building, her aggressiveness now rose toward her new supervisor. Betty felt that this woman acted unfairly in not releasing her on time for our interviews. "After all I started with you before, and that keeps me out of trouble anyway." She had now advanced far enough to see that her reaction revealed how she tied herself to little things from the past, following her habits like a slave instead of thinking how she might handle things better in the present and future. Yet that supervisor was "just too demanding."

In order to avoid talking back and showing anger, Betty went out to talk to the dog or went to the cellar to "cool off." However, within ten days she spoke of that supervisor and the whole institution as a "blessing in disguise." "They give you a hard time, but they make you grow and learn things I never wanted to learn before. It's rough, but it's good."

In summary, Betty abandoned her senselessly exaggerated expressions of hostility, and her inordinate desire for love, for an existence guided by relative reasonableness and by acceptance of social values and responsibility.

She was still holding an office job a year after parole, and no adverse reports on her had been received.

Test Changes

MMPI: L 46-36, Mf (63-76), At (11-16), R (6-12), Jh 26-19
16PF: A (7-4), E 2-6, Q2 5-10, Q3 5-8, Q4 5-2
HGI: B 8-5, D (2-5), H 9-6
HOW: Tr 120-82, Cr 64-63

Betty achieved some solid gains in reducing the hostility and guilt that had disturbed her equilibrium in the past. She may be less likely to follow her sexual impulses blindly. She was not as restless as she had been before therapy, and had come to realize that identifying herself with delinquent groups in order to reduce her inner discomfort and insecurity would only produce greater inner and outer pressures. Having resolved some tensions she was better able to function as a responsible worker, as her teachers' ratings might be taken to indicate.

Cora

Age 18, 22 interviews in three months. Oldest in a large family. Committed for promiscuity, truancy, running away from home, incorrigibility, and stealing.

Cora was quite reticent in the first two interviews. Pauses were long. She said she was embarrassed to have to speak to a stranger about her life, "but my life was a mess anyway." She readily answered my questions about what brought her to the institution. She lived for parties and drinking. She was forced into sex the first time; then, later, let many boys have her. She could not understand it. Once when she was on the run from home and a fellow approached her she threatened to stab him with a pair of scissors she had grabbed to protect herself. She meant it, and he did not bother her any more. Yet she later just let herself go sexually with many boys although she "felt rotten afterward." She cried about herself. She crossed the street if she saw a boy with whom she had been intimate and avoided looking at him. If she liked a boy, she wouldn't let him touch her because she "wanted him to respect her."

A wide split between sexual drives and self-respect and super-ego had developed in her. She apparently used sex for self-destruction rather than gratification.

As she sat silent in the third interview I asked, "What is the problem you want me to help you with?" She poured out her tale of woe, uncovering the potent antecedents for her present and future maladjustment.

"My problem was that I was born. That sounds stupid. I don't mean that I don't want to live. . . . I wonder sometimes how things would be if I wasn't here. . . . I know my mother would be heart-

50

broken. Dad, too. Others might say, 'good riddance.' . . . What bothers me is I don't feel much for my family when they aren't around me, though I like them when I see them. I feel as if I'm a burden to them when I ask for some clothing. . . . When they aren't here, I think bad things about them. . . .Mother always worked. I know she had to, to keep us children alive when Dad left us. We had baby-sitters. Mother was never around when I needed her. I was about seven or eight then. I used to go to a minister in the neighborhood. They wanted to adopt me. I went everywhere with them. They gave me the same allowance as they gave their own children. . . . Later I saw mother and the minister flirting. . . . He got divorced from his wife later on. I didn't like him for this. . . . Some men used to come to our house. I slept with Mom then. She'd ask me if I'd sleep with my sister. I knew why, and I wouldn't. She went with that man to the kitchen and slept with him on the floor. I kept crying. Wanted to get away from it all."

I tried to provide emotional support by saying: "It scared you —what you saw happening." She apparently failed to grasp my intention, but took the words literally.

"I didn't need to see. I could hear all right. . . . Later, when we left that place, she flirted with my stepfather, and he left his family. He was nine years younger than Mom, eleven years older than me. I didn't like him kissing me. . . . Sam, her old lover, still used to come to see Mom. She'd get a phone call in the middle of ironing. 'I'll go out for a walk,' she'd say. She'd comb her hair and go. I'd go around the block trying to find her, but I couldn't. I was unhappy. She would come back after two or three hours. Her hair'd be messed up. She looked real happy, and before she was grouchy. . . . I felt really hurt when she named a clay turtle I made for her 'Sam.' There I was showing her my love that way, and she gave it such a name!

"Later, I started messing up. She'd tell me to be good but wouldn't do anything about it. If I came in after midnight she wouldn't say much, though she told me before to be home at eleven. Sometimes she threatened me with the police. I went out deliberately to see if she really cared, but she wouldn't do anything. Finally she took me to court. . . . I wonder what you think of my mom now. She isn't sexy-looking, quite plain . . . [crying] like me. . . ."

51

I was moved and tried to reassure her. "Children need not be like parents and they are not judged by their parents."

She smiled through her tears. "Thank you, Doctor."

She lost her tenseness in the interviews, although she was always rather reticent. Being aware of the traumas she had suffered in interpersonal relationships I respected her silences and did not try to modify her guardedness. She explained her shyness by her belief that everyone thought she was no good, and she knew it herself. I sometimes had to probe and ask questions in order to understand her clearly. There were long pauses. She once said that some girls had said that I could read thoughts, and she was trying not to think because she had bad thoughts and didn't want me to know.

I already knew too many bad things about her and her mother; I was probably disgusted with her only I couldn't show it. I sensed that a sexual transference was behind her wonderings and uneasiness. Considering it therapeutically wiser not to recognize these feelings for what they were I let her repress them. I tried to reassure her about her acceptability as a person and used her discomfort to teach her a more successful way of handling "bad" thoughts than denying their existence. I urged her to be honest with herself and to accept both bad and good thoughts as part of human nature; and instead of torturing herself about bad thoughts, to feel pride in not yielding to them.

She reported that she was doing better in school, was more interested in her subjects, and was not talking so much during class periods. She had not been able to stop herself from chattering before because she "felt so restless and didn't care." Now she thought of trying to go to college if she could get over her "laziness."

After a visit from her mother, she joyfully reported that she no longer was angry with her. "Both of us were bad before, but we're trying to be good now. I want to be a decent person, like you or Miss P. [superintendent] or Mrs. K. [cottage counselor]." Apparently her identifications became more aspiring as her guilt feelings lightened.

She disliked wearing glasses because she imagined they made her even less attractive; she thought of herself as an ugly, skinny creature. I pointed out her unfairness to herself because she was quite a good-looking girl. She indirectly asked for repeated assurances about her looks. Finally she reported that wearing glasses didn't bother her anymore.

She had been angry with herself for being a "cry baby." When counselors or one of the girls said something critical about her, she had not been able to prevent tears. Now she didn't mind if someone contradicted or criticized her, so long as she felt that she was right. Obviously her anxieties were reduced as guilt and self-disgust receded into the background. Some girls actually told her they liked her better now. "I don't hate myself as before, and people like me better now. I was behaving like a two-year-old idiot before." She reported, and her cottage counselor confirmed, that she was not as quarrelsome as previously.

During several interviews she was troubled about how to tell her mother that she wanted to go to workhome before she returned to her own home because she believed the old temptations might be too strong in her hometown. "Before I was only fooling around. But now I want to stay away from fun that lasts only for a while and then gives you trouble." Finally Cora brought herself to tell her mother about her feelings, felt better for it, and went to a workhome.

The reports of her first three months in the workhome were satisfactory. She was doing well in school. Then she ran away, and was returned to the institution three months later. After six weeks, Cora sent me a note asking if I could spare time to see her. I asked: "Why didn't you call me when you were feeling upset, before you ran away. I told you that you could, at any time."

She cried bitterly during the inteview. Her explanation once more supported the conviction I had developed in working with these disturbed youngsters, i.e., that psychotherapy should be continued in the first few months of life in the community.

"I didn't like that lady. She was grouchy, and her kids spoke nasty to me. There was no orderliness in that home like we get used to having here, but I was trying to take it. I missed school one day. The other girls were signing year books that day, and I didn't have one. Then I was afraid to go so school. I thought of calling you, but I was afraid you'd think I was stupid, because what bothered me was stupid. I ran away, got me a job, then lost it. Started shacking with a guy. I didn't care for him but I wanted to get pregnant, wanted to ruin myself. Then I left him and went to Mother, and she brought me back here. When I was with you I wanted to make something of myself. But then I lose courage, and I get to feel that I don't care any more."

Psychotherapy with Cora had been only partially successful. It freed her from a thorough rejection of herself and from the crippling feelings of anxiety and guilt. Although not yet firmly entrenched in a new and hopeful concept of herself she had experienced the rewarding feelings of living according to her best lights, and it may be expected that these will serve in good stead when her self-destructive drives threaten again.

Test Changes

MMPI: *F* 66-53, *Hs* 56-42, *Pd* 81-64, *Pt* 69-58, *Sc* 71-51, *A* 28-17, *At* 29-20, *De* 38-33, *Do* 10-15, *Ho* 33-25, *Ad* 19-25, *So-r* (19-25)
16PF: *A* 3-6, *C* 3-6, *L* 8-5, *O* 8-3, *Q3* 3-6, *Q4* 10-5
HGI: *Ho* 55-35, *C* 10-6, *D* 5-2, *F* 9-3
HOW: *Tr* 61-58, *Cr* (82½-89)

The main test changes confirm the clinical impression that Cora's nonconforming, inappropriate, hostile behavior was not likely to occur so persistently as it did in the past. Agitation and overemotional reactions were no longer the hallmarks of her response to environment. She became less irritable and spiteful, and no longer viewed others with strong suspiciousness. She was better able to get along without being misled through lack of self-confidence, more decisive and less subject to vacillation, and her ego was freer from hampering conflicts.

Her running away from the workhome might be explained by lack of emotional support, overwhelming feelings of inferiority when comparing herself with the "good" girls of her new school, and the subsequent revival of self-destructive trends.

Dora

Age 14, IQ bright normal, 37 interviews in seven months. Strikingly beautiful. Committed for running away and being incorrigible at home and school. Referred for therapy after five months in the institution.

She was unrelenting in her struggle against a strict elderly cottage counselor and a young woman teacher. Her explanations of her hostility toward them were irrational and contradictory. When I pointed out these contradictions, she admitted impatiently: "I'm so mixed up." She manifested many signs of anxiety: rigid posture, stretching of arms and torso to relieve tension, pushing and often blurred speech, and cold perspiring hands. This tenseness persisted during the first dozen interviews. Later she became giggly, said that she wanted to talk with me because she could not be near her mother, with whom she had shared all her troubles. This was a fantasy; the actual relationship was one of rejection.

Soon she reported that when she was angry and wanted to strike out in some way she would tell herself. "Don't do it. Dr. Ray wants you to be good." On another occasion she explained: "I'm glad I talk with you. You knock some sense into my head. Yesterday, I started moving furniture in the room to pile it against the door, then I said to myself. 'What are you doing this for?' 'Because I want to,' I answered. 'Don't be a fool,' I told myself. At other times I might have gone on with it, but now I said: 'Dora, behave!' And I put the things quietly back so Mrs. Z. wouldn't see I was messing up the room."

Such manipulation might have saved her from some aggressive excesses but did not always help her to avoid clashes in the classroom and in the cottage. She developed an intense attachment to the superintendent and yearned for closeness with her; she admired her character, firmness, and religious convictions. Dora began to try to control her agitation by turning to religion, in emulation of the superintendent. All these maneuvers appeared, in the course of interviews, as defenses against devastating guilt feelings. The intimation of this came in a repeated dream reported early in therapy. In the dream, Dora would be taken to heaven, where she waited with others to enter. But before the gate opened for her, she would wake up in terror. I supported her in developing clearer religious convictions.

One day a loud scream from the classroom penetrated my closed door. Dora was calling me. When I entered the classroom, she was in one corner of the room, and the teacher and the girls in the other with overturned desks between them. Dora followed me to her room. We spoke for a while; and apparently quieted, she promised to lie down and rest or sleep.

55

An hour later the counselor on duty knocked on my door: Dora was trying to kill herself. She had piled the mattress and furniture against the door, and no one was able to enter the room. As I approached the wing in which Dora's room was located I could hear shrill cries of "I want to die! I want to die!"

Through the observation window I saw Dora standing in one corner, twisting and tightening a string around her neck. It did not take much talking to induce her to remove the obstacles and let me into the room. We straightened the room together, then sat talking for a while. She was "ashamed of this foolishness." I promised an interview the next day. In the interview I pressed her to reveal the reasons for her recent upset. She finally broke down, sobbing.

Her father had had intercourse with her the first time when she was ten years old. (Her mother had previously described how Dora's father would come home drunk and ask Dora who was then only six, to kiss him repeatedly on the mouth and urged her to do it more passionately each time.) When her mother later remarried, Dora rebelled against her stern stepfather and ran off to her father; he was then living in an eastern state. He came home drunk one night, called her by Dora's mother's name and slept with her. "I felt a duty to give in to him. He was poor, and was still trying to buy food and clothes for me. Also he told me that if I was not with him in that one room he would've been able to have a whore there for himself. This hurt me the most."

She would bring a boy friend of hers to sleep in the room on a couch so that her father would not molest her. She had never told anyone about it, and had not dared to tell me before. "This has been making me do these crazy things here. . . . Oh, how ugly! . . . I don't know what I'd do without you here."

I repeated then, also in later interviews, that neither man nor God would hold her responsible for what her father had led her into as a child; that only from now on, since she was more grown up, could she be partly responsible for such happenings; that she was not the only girl with whom a father had committed incest, for I knew of at least two others in the institution. On leaving the office, Dora seemed sufficiently calmed to ask: "Are your eardrums O.K. after all that screaming I did last night?" Apparently her ego was strong enough to help her recover her poise quickly.

56

A week later she was on a rampage again. Her voice was hoarse but quite strong. Tightening her dress belt around her neck she was sitting on the floor yelling: "I want to die. . . . I hate this damn hole. . . . I'll be dead soon." Again I persuaded her easily to remove the dresser so I could enter the room. Her explanation of her tantrum was irrelevant and irrational, involving some petty gossip about her. "But I'm no good anyway. No one loves me. Mother hasn't come to see me. If I was any good I wouldn't be here."

I proposed to take her to the institutional hospital for a few days of rest. She followed meekly, saying how difficult it would be to face the nurse, whom she respected greatly. I told her that her mother had called me the day before to ask about her. "What did Mother say?" I was blunt in order to challenge her to make a stronger effort to improve: 'She is worried that you may be going crazy because you are doing these things. I told her you were not crazy at all, but you were just refusing to grow up."

Dora enjoyed her "internment" in the hospital "punishment room," where she was placed because no other room was available. "They can keep me here the next eight months, and I'll still be the same."

"What might help you?"

"When people try to understand me, like you do. I wasn't going to open my door last time, no matter what punishment they threatened me with. But you came and told me there's a more sensible way to do things, and I calmed down. [I had said nothing of the sort on that occasion.] People don't understand how hard it is to grow up. You want to keep near people who took care of you in your childhood and be without worries. You don't want to grow up and be independent and have to be responsible for everything. It's not easy to be a teen-ager, but they think we're all bad." She had enough insight to see that her tantrums arose from her fear of assuming adult responsibilities.

Dora threatened violence if she were returned to her cottage. In the next interview, dealing with her stubbornness, I proposed that we role-play a little. I played Dora, and she played the superintendent who was listening to her "arguments." After a while, the stopped me: "Oh, I don't sound like that, do I?" After a few days she returned to her cottage willingly.

She brought a poem to the following interview and put the

paper face down on my desk, asking me to read it after she left. She had titled the poem, "A Man I Know." It is worth quoting because it expresses the transference reaction of many of the girls in therapy:

"A man I know is sweet and kind,
When I'm in trouble I always find,
He's there to help you at any time,
And best of all God made his help mine.

Whether I'm happy, or whether I'm sad,
I love him more every day,
And his name is Doctor Ray."

In another outburst of rage in the classroom she broke four chairs. "I'm ashamed of it now," she told me. "I first kicked one chair against the wall. Then I didn't know what was happening: I was shoving chairs around and wondering why I was doing it. I felt better, though, after it, because I got it off my chest." She also felt better because she was receiving the punishment demanded by her still-unresolved guilt feelings. She also seemed to allow herself these rages in order to experience a transient omnipotence in compensation for devastating feeling of worthlessness.

A week later she wondered how she could have been good for so long. "I could've blown my top on one occasion, but I changed my mind. I find they're good to me when I'm good. I wrote to Miss P. that I really didn't hate this cottage like I used to say."

"You feel like a good girl now, don't you?"

"Yes, the past doesn't bother me any more. I'm looking toward the future."

She told about a long, hard sleep of the day before. It sounded like a cathartic, tranquilizing experience for her. I asked if she had ever had such an experience before. "Only once, when my parents separated. That was the greatest blow of my life. I felt as if a piece of me was cut off, like my arm was cut off. We were a happy family before that. I couldn't understand mother then. . . . I remember, I had to go to sleep. It was noontime. When I woke up it was already dark. I don't know what happens with me when I sleep like that. I have no dreams. But I feel better."

58

Dora was actively writing poetry in this phase. She dedicated several poems to me. In one of these, which she called "Never Give Up," but later changed the title, she tells of her despair and hope, of her longing to see her "cup," emptied by the destructive experiences of her life, filled with refreshing, reviving, optimistic feelings. (The poem provided the title for this volume and is reproduced as its epigraph to symbolize the struggle of these traumatized girls for a satisfying way of life.)

However, Dora could not permanently retain the buoyant outlook of her poem. The old, desperate feelings would return to flood her with anxiety. She turned her longings toward God, the consolation of lonely and frightened minds. In the poem "Does Anyone Care?" she tells of her flight from loveless depression toward sunny horizons of religious experience:

"Does anyone care if you live or die?
Does anyone care if you laugh or cry?
Just think of the One up above,
Who is endlessly watching with mercy and love.

When skies are gloomy, and the darkness gray,
That is the time for you to pray
For God's helping hand, throughout the day,
In his kind and gentle loving way.

So even if your heart is full of sin,
Open it up and let Him in.
Then say to yourself a little prayer.
And you'll soon know that someone does care!"

One day she came to the interview with large scratches on her face and arms. She tried to turn away from me in order to hide the signs of her self-hatred. "I don't care, anyway. Life is nothing to me."

I must have felt despondent about her progress, for I asked: "Is my time with you wasted, Dora?"

"No, you helped me feel better. I can think better, but I still don't care."

"You're muddling yourself again. If you really did not care you wouldn't be so angry when people disappoint you."

59

"My life is messed up, anyway. It will be short at the rate I go hating myself because one day they won't stop me. . . . I'll end in hell anyway. I'm no good."

She spoke of how she could not forget the bad things she had done. I repeated my former assurances about her not being responsible for childhood mistakes because she again seemed overwhelmed by self-contempt. I had sensed her need correctly, for she reported at the following interview: "I was mad with you [smile]. After I left you last time I cried and cried, more than ever. And I couldn't get mad with girls, though I wanted to. . . . Oh, I hate to speak about this, but you helped me. Sure it was hard to look at the smashed idol for the second time—I mean about my father . . . but you made me feel good. Ever since I spoke with you about that thing I was trying in vain to forget, I feel so much lighter—as if ten pounds fell off my head."

She reached to touch my hand in gratitude but did not complete the movement. Instead she proposed a new plan for interviews. She wondered whether I would see her without regular appointments by calling her in once a week. "I will not have you to help me to be good outside. I have to start being independent. Also, it'll help me be good all week if I don't know when you'll call me to your office. Otherwise I try to be good only before regular appointments." I had obviously become her parent and her conscience.

In the following two months she valiantly held her temper, although she was often close to a tantrum. Once when she felt angry, she told me, she hid under the bed and hit her mattress with her fist; when screams welled up from within, she held her jaws tight with her hands so that no sound would escape.

I called her to my office after she had spent a week at her home. She was happy that she could get along with her stepfather; she could see that he ordered her about for her own good.

"Why couldn't you do it before?"

"I was blind, just thought everything had to be my way. . . . But you people here showed me you cared for me. You, Miss P. (superintendent), Mr. T. (assistant superintendent). Before I thought that no one thought I was any good."

In summary, through psychotherapy Dora had been snatched from a course of progressive maladjustment, seeking of punishment and self-destruction. If she had not been unburdened of her

60

crushing guilt over incest she would have ended in psychosis, as many such cases do. Her struggle led to the release of her creative capacities and a reorganization of her chaotic emotions.

Three months after being discharged on parole Dora called me: Did I think she should get married? She said she was already in the home of a fifteen-year-old boy; they loved each other; and his parents loved her. The marriage was approved by parole authorities, and was still enduring a year later.

Test Changes

MMPI: *Hs* (38-52)
16PF: *A* 4-9, *L* 8-4, *Q1* 3-8, *Q4* 6-2
HGI: *Ho* 28-15, *C* 6-1, *G* 5-2, *H* 8-3
How: *Tr* (80-94.5), *Cr* (100.5-105)

The test results do not indicate marked changes in Dora's personality. Her conscious hostility and suspiciousness had abated and she became less restless. Her ability to use the problem-solving approach increased as she was less threatened by her feelings. Her guilt feelings, a crucial upsetting factor in the past, were less intense. No wonder that teachers and counselors rated her poorly after all the disturbances she had caused.

Emma

Age 17, dull normal mentality, 25 interviews in four months. Five months in the institution before being referred to the therapist.

She had run away from the institution, spent her usual three to four weeks in her room and seemed to be getting progressively lost in some sort of daze and confusion. In the early interviews she was silent, tense, apprehensive, and doubted that I could help her. "It didn't do any good when I saw a psychiatrist when I was ten or eleven. Then I saw a social worker at the City Hospital. I liked her. But she started seeing me less often after a while, and I didn't like it. She also started asking me questions about how I felt about my mom and I didn't want to see her any more. I wish I hadn't stopped. Maybe I wouldn't be here now, and maybe I wouldn't have done all those stupid things I did."

She cried softly, hiding her face, refusing the tissues I offered her. "But I don't know what to do with myself. I wish I was never born. I want to be good, but I can't. I've done more low things than many old people did in all their life." She preferred to come once instead of twice a week, as I offered, because then she would not appear to others so crazy and so in need of help.

Emma was filled with self-disgust. Her conscience tormented her with many real and imagined misdeeds. She had never gotten along with her mother after the latter had remarried several years earlier. It was Emma who had caused her mother to go to a hospital for six months of psychiatric treatment, and it was she who had broken up her mother's second marriage. She had caused the death of her grandma three years previously. Although her grandmother had cancer and asthma, Emma was convinced it was her misbehavior that killed her.

She had disgraced herself by drinking. She had had some sexual experiences, but only when she was drunk. It was disgusting for her to remember how she had run after a law student, going to his room and offering herself. He hadn't touched her, instead he had spoken kindly to her about the necessity to stop drinking. She had senselessly run away from home, from foster homes, Juvenile Hall, and from the institution. She imagined that she was "going crazy" and that her head was empty anyway because she didn't listen to her mother, who wanted her to study and go to college. She felt "so stupid" when she talked with others, and hated her fat body, "like a blimp," and her buck teeth. She didn't dare smile in order not to bare her teeth. (As a matter of fact, she was not much overweight and had quite attractive features.) Obviously she had shifted to her body her own disgust with her behavior.

Her trust in human beings had been severely shaken. She would force herself to talk for a while about her troubled feelings and then stop suddenly, asking why she had told me that. She was uneasy about revealing her feelings to anyone. Apparently two other girls in her cottage—both in therapy with me at that time —had been urging her to face her problems and not to be so fearful in interviews. On one occasion, she asked in earnest apprehension: "Can you read my thoughts?" When I answered that I was trying to understand her as a person but depended on her explanations all the time, she expressed her further sus-

62

picion: "But if you don't read my thoughts, how could you tell me some things about myself that I didn't tell you about?"

She seemed to be fighting a developing sense of trust in me. On another occasion she wondered: "Don't you get tired and bored listening to girls' troubles? Is this job just a job to you, or is it more?" I interpreted her words as an expression of her inner debate over whether to trust me.

She reported some improvements in self-control. She had found a cigarette and thrown it away although she had wanted to smoke it; she had chosen to obey the school rules. A girl had stolen Emma's bottle of perfume and drank it, and Emma had kept her temper. She had intended to drink it herself sometime but was testing her will power by postponing the "kick." She had stopped most of her nibbling between meals and talking in the kitchen, which had gotten her into trouble with cottage counselors before. She was not moved to tears as often as previously.

She used these improvements as indications that she no longer needed interviews. She pretended lightheartedness, but her sad smile belied this. I asked questions about her true mood, and she hung her head. Each interview in which she broke through with "confessions" was followed by one of reestablishment of repressive defenses and emotional distance. "I want to forget those things."

I would remark: "But you are going about it the wrong way. You can't forget by force. You failed in that before. You have to face troublesome thoughts."

The repetitious reply was "I do not want to."

After eight interviews she sent me a note: "Since I do not feel that I am gaining anything from our interviews, I have decided to discontinue my visits to your office. I appreciate your efforts to help me. Thank you." I sent her a note suggesting that she might come back later if she wanted to.

Three days later she ran away from the institution. It was a cold, snowy night and she was tracked down by her footsteps and caught approximately two miles away from the cottage. She scratched her wrists and her neck with a needle in symbolic suicide. I asked the cottage counselor to tell Emma that I was willing to see her when she felt like it. "I might just as well see him now," had been her indifferent answer.

I saw her in the cottage. She pretended to be bashful about her scars, hiding them pointedly. Then she would "forget " and put her arm on the desk or raise her head in thought so that I would be able to see the marks on her neck plainly. She cried, condemning herself: "I hate myself for letting Mrs. D. down. That's what I do to my friends. She trusted me, and I failed her by running away. She could've lost her job too. I would rather be in a jail than in the cottage because I can't face Mrs. K. now. She thought I was getting better."

I pointed out that she was again underselling herself, just as she did before with her teeth, sins, fatness. She nodded and smiled. I asked: "Do you want to see me again?"

"I feel better after talking with you, but Mrs. K. will say: 'Who does she think she is to have Dr. Ray come to see her in the cottage?' "

"Whose feelings are more important for you—yours or other people's?"

"I guess mine."

"Why didn't you want to come to talk with me last week?"

"I thought you were only making an effort to see me. . . . You pitied me."

I reaffirmed my faith in her worth as a person. She asked if I could see her twice a week now. I understood that I was no longer a threat to her. Then her thoughts began to turn more often toward the future: the work that she would do, the church to which she wanted to return. Past memories occasionally overwhelmed her but she did not hate herself so intensely, and her remorse became moderate. She found it helpful to read and practice N. V. Peale's *Power of Positive Thinking,* which I had given her. The present situation became more tolerable to her. She saw that it benefited her to be in the institution for a while to gain control of herself. Her feelings toward her mother became less bitter; she now saw that she had hurt her mother by her spitefulness, and felt that the two of them could clear up conflicts by talking instead of fighting.

She also discovered that the girls were not teasing her as much as before because she tried not to hurt their feelings. She became panicky when assigned to wait on the officers' table, but later reported that she was no longer afraid of making a few mistakes. When a counselor caught her eating a cookie, Emma apologized but did not brood over the "dire consequences" as she used to.

She then began stewing about one of the cottage counselors,

feeling that the latter was too strict and never praised her, and expressed a desire to lock her in a room and feed her onions until she became deathly sick. Then Emma showed anxiety: "It's awful to feel so cruel." She seemed surprised to hear me say that it is human to feel angry and mean occasionally.

Later she had conflicts with an excitable, mentally limited girl who was unjustly accusing Emma to the cottage counselors. Emma denied any angry feelings, recognizing only that she was distressed. At my prodding, she came to accept her anger as normal. This was the first interview in which she thanked me upon leaving. In the following interview she spoke of her surprise at her ability to be angry and not retaliate directly. "Before, I only wanted to have my own way." I explained that she was becoming more mature. She glanced at me in pleased disbelief.

She became upset when another girl told her that she went to talk with me because she was crazy. Emma's mother had told her that she would end up in an insane asylum if she did not get hold of herself. In the same interview she mentioned that "some girls are hung on you, but I won't come to feel that way." I sensed that her old fears of closeness and the resulting hurt had revived within her because of her sexual feelings. I deliberately glossed over the underlying meaning of her communication in order not to threaten her with recognition of her feelings. Emma interpreted this as a sign of my disinterest in her as a female. She expressed her reaction in a veiled way by speaking of Mrs. R., whose favorite Emma had been for a while until she was rejected.

Technically, the noninterpretation of the sexual transference was probably a mistake, for this was the last interview to which Emma came. On the other hand I was afraid that her ego was too fragile to stand a confrontation with the threatening situation. Anyway, Emma sent a note the next day:

"Dear Dr. Ray: Would you please not call me to your office from now on. I would like to see how things would go without our interviews. I hope I am not making a mistake. But I think I can get along without counseling. I've been talking to you since November, and it seems to me that it has been a waste of time. I think there are girls that you can help more than me.

You probably think I am running away from someone that is trying to help me, or I just don't want to face what is bothering me. This may be true. I don't know. But I can't help the way I feel.

65

Please do me the favor and not mention this to anyone. Thank you."

In summary, Emma benefited only moderately from psychotherapy in the institution. She could not overcome her fear of emotional closeness, was threatened by the only way of loving she knew, that is the sexual experience, and used her habitual way of handling uncomfortable situations by escaping—discontinuing the contacts.

Six months later, when on parole, Emma called me: she was worried about what she was doing and wanted my help. She expressed regret that she had not gone on with her interviews. "Probably, I wouldn't be in the mess I'm in now." She had gone back to drinking, though only a few times; she was not able to get along with her mother; she had quit school; she was afraid that her parole would be revoked. Now she seemed determined to try more responsible ways of behavior. I saw her in one interview, and her anxiety seemed abated. The last report I had about her was that she had married, seemed happy, and had left the state with her husband, a salesman.

Test Changes

MMPI: *D* 59-36, *Hy* 61-37, *Pd* 79-53, *Mf* 53-41, *Pa* 79-59, *Pt* 81-55, *Sc* 69-49, *Si* 64-51, *A* 26-12, *At* 34-13, *Es* 38-48, *Dq* 17-10, *De* 27-20, *Do* 10-16, *Ca* 20-10, *Rec* 15-9, *Jh* 13-8, *Ho* 15-8, *Ad* 22-31, *So-r* (24-31)
16PF: *C* 6-10, *H* 5-10
HGI: *Ho* 25-11, *C* 6-2, *F* 5-0, *H* 6-3
HOW: *Tr* 58-58, *Cr* 105-102.5

The tests portray a considerable lessening of neurotic trends in Emma. Her mood became better as she became less anxiety-ridden. More secure about her person, she was therefore more capable of satisfying relationships with others. She relinquished her intense suspicions of other people, became less hostile, and overpowering guilt feelings caused fewer tensions. Her orientation to reality was more appropriate. Greater emotional stability allowed her to detach her attention from her own woes, real or imagined. Thus, with tensions reduced, she had less need to seek relief in acting out. Her dependency needs were not so powerful

66

and her ability to remain a person in her own right in spite of environmental pressures was increased, so that it may be expected that she will not revert consistently to finding relief in alcohol.

Fay

Age 17, bright normal IQ, 27 interviews in four months. She had apparently been too hastily committed by the judge for incorrigibility and running away from home, without prior probation, probably because she had just moved into the community from out of state, had been saucy with the social worker, and might have looked burly and dangerous because of her large size.

Fay seemed to be the only "normal" confused teen-ager in the experimental group. Her parents were together, and although they allowed her some freedom they had retained definite controls over her. She had enjoyed the closeness of friends and relatives in a rural area in the Mid-West. She had been popular in school, a cheerleader, and a member of the girls' basketball team; she also played the piano, and was always among the top three students in her class.

Her experience in the institution marked her first separation from her parents. The "running away" had apparently been for two days, and on the second day Fay had called her mother to tell her that she had slept at a friend's home. Her institutionalization came as a shock. She seemed unable to pay attention to instructions, and could not be motivated to follow the training routine. She escaped, but was caught near her home a hundred miles away. It was at this time that she was referred to me. She cried copiously against the injustice of the commitment; things were becoming unreal to her, and she was afraid that she was going crazy.

Much of the interview time was spent in listening to her. When her anxiety was somewhat reduced she became quite chatty and spoke about the good times she had had with friends and family. One of her amusing communications was that in the three months before coming to the institution she had had seventeen marriage proposals, nine of them serious. But she had refused them all, for she wanted to finish school and be a secretary. She felt rejected by institutional authorities, and it seemed to her that I was the only person interested in her. She had been close to her dad, and now she found a substitute in me. She confided her ambivalence toward two boys, as well as her jealousy. I used my influence to motivate her to be more orderly, and to use her time in the institution for schooling.

Since no signs of serious emotional maladjustment appeared after a dozen interviews, I asked her whether she still wanted to come twice a week or only once. She wanted to go on without change for at least five more weeks. "I don't know how I might get to feel. I might mess up again. Sometimes I despise myself for being here. I won't be able to look other people straight in the eye because they'll know I was in a reform school." I suggested that she try to make the best of an unpleasant situation. She did not adopt the suggestion, judging by the reactions of counselors who continued to punish her for the covert uncooperativeness revealed in her sloppy and careless appearance and habits. She was apparently continuing her old struggle with her mother and enjoying it. I did not wish to move her toward submissiveness because I felt it was healthy to resist undeserved frustrations. However, I continued to remind her that she should follow the regulations carefully to avoid trouble. Her grades in cottage work were improving.

In summary, Fay seemed to require emotional support more than she needed to be pushed toward radical changes. It is probably for that reason that there were no dramatic moments in her contact with me. Her main gain seemed to be in lessened despair and anxiety.

She left the state with her parents after being released on parole. She writes regularly to her parole agent, reporting good success at school and happiness in family cicumstances.

Test Changes

MMPI: *Hs* 76-50, *D* 73-59, *Hy* 80-63, *Pt* 78-63, *A* 19-10, *At* 24-17, *Es* 40-46, *Ca* 18-10, *Rec* (3-10)
16PF: *I* 4-8, *M* 5-10, *Q4* (2-5)
HGI: *A* 7-1, *C* (1-4), *H* (4-7)
HOW: *Tr* 86-72, *Cr* (87.5-107)

Fay's neurotic components were decidedly brought within normal limits. In some ways her rigid control of her impulses appeared to be loosened, so that she might be expected to act somewhat less responsibly. The negative evaluation of the cottage counselors may point to her poorer compliance with the demands of authority. She became more irritable and tense even though her anxiety level and excitability had been reduced. Her attitude of opposition to authority figures was still in evidence, with a resultant increase in guilt feelings. However, her adaptive ability had grown, so that this rebelliousness should not lead to serious excesses in behavior.

Grace

Age 17, dull normal intelligence, 27 interviews in five months.

She asked for the first interview. She started crying even before she sat down, manifesting intense guilt feelings and self-contempt. "I don't know what to do. I know you helped other girls; I hope you'll help me. I can't get my parents off my mind. That's all I think about: how good they were to me, and how bad I was to them. I wouldn't listen when father told me not to drink. He was good; he didn't want to hit me. I wish he had. I wouldn't come home when I was told. They spent one hundred dollars for lawyers trying to keep me out of here. It was all my fault. They tell me they miss me and are looking forward to my coming home. The judge told them I'd be here six months. How can I tell them I'll be here a year? Oh, I hate myself! And I'm so snappy with the girls here. I talk rudely to them even if they're kind to me. I can't stand to be locked up in that room at night. Mrs. K. told me that she'd move me to one of those front rooms if I don't stop quarreling with other girls. And I hate those front rooms even more. I don't like being so hateful with the girls, but I can't stand them. If I could talk with you, maybe I'd be better. . . . When my parents come, I can't let them leave. I'm so unhappy to see them go. I see them in my dreams. I cry when I wake up. I'm afraid something is going to happen to them. Dad isn't in good health, and he worries about me. I don't want anything to happen to him when I am not there. I quarreled with my brother in the afternoon, and he got killed in a car wreck that evening. I wish I could tell him that I was sorry."

Apparently the other girls enjoyed baiting Grace. One girl called her a prostitute. "I was mad, because I wasn't a bad girl. A doctor examined me and told my parents I was still a virgin." Another girl spread the rumor that Grace had poured her chamber pot through the window. Grace almost got into a fight with her.

I reminded Grace that boys tease angry dogs by poking sticks through the fence; if the dog disregards them, the boys leave him alone. "I'll try to do the same," she said. Her quarrels became less frequent although she remained basically hostile to most of her peers. Probably the jealous and over-sensitive pattern was established by her being the youngest in the family of four children.

Another front on which she was battling for mastery over affective drives was her attachment to Paul, her boy friend. In the beginning she had vowed to stick to him no matter what her parents, the judge, or the parole officers might say. She hated the judge for forbidding correspondence with Paul. Gradually, over a number of interviews, her attitude changed. Paul became less important in her fantasies, and restitution to her parents and plans for finishing high school came to be her main concerns.

She saw that Paul had many faults: a spoiled only child, wild, drinking, and so emotionally unstable that the judge had ordered him to take a psychiatric examination. Occasionally he had been rude and inconsiderate to her, although she had been ready to accept regular beatings. He was also good to her, and protected her from other boys. She still tingled with delight when thinking of the deep closeness she had felt toward him when they lay in an overturned car and he asked tenderly, "Are you hurt, honey?" He and his friend had rolled the car for the thrill of it, disregarding her pleas to slow down.

Now she saw that her state of mind at that time was one of perpetual drunkenness with thrills and artificial excitement. She laughed at the feelings of importance she had had when she rode on the back seat of the motorcycle, awfully proud of her leather jacket and the roar of motors in the sleepy town. They had enjoyed defying the "cops," but now Grace was sorry for not being more respectful to authorities. "When I get out I won't be going with that wild crowd. They are just like children. I'll try to find nice girls to go with."

She dreamed of being approached by her former friends and telling them she no longer cared for the fun they offered. She felt that Paul would also need to talk with someone to get some sense into his head—someone like me, otherwise she expected he would only get worse and end up in the penitentiary.

Her voice, her posture, the content of her communications indicated clearly that Grace was relating to me as a father substitute. She would speak quickly and somewhat indistinctly, like a little girl embarrassed by her naughtiness, and promise that she would try harder to be good, and to satisfy the cottage counselors and teachers. She spoke proudly of praise received from others, and of holding her temper when she felt like fighting and speaking angry words. She was sorry she hadn't listened to her dad, and she now tried earnestly to please me. She felt grieved when a teacher told her that her talks with me did not seem to be doing her much good because she had been excessively talkative in the classroom one day.

Grace spoke of disagreeing with her parents' view, expressed on their most recent visit, that it was their fault she had gone wrong; she was emphatic in claiming the fault as hers, the result of her failure to listen to grown-ups. Now she was ashamed of the rudeness other girls showed to institutional personnel, and felt embarrassed when some girls did not behave like young ladies during their visit to a sorority house on a university campus. "I used to be like that. I didn't care. But now I don't want to let people down. And most of all I don't want to hurt my folks."

After several interviews which began with reports of how good she had been, I asked her why she mentioned these things to me. She explained: "You've helped me to be good. I feel better after talking with you. Mrs. C. tells me you helped me. I'm trying to act my age. Girls call me "chicken" and "square" because I'm trying to be good. I stay away from them. They'll learn too. I like Mrs. S. now, and you know how I hated her before. The other day I was amused at Mrs. L. for griping at us in the class all the time; she used to get me awful mad before. Also, because I'm not hateful to the girls, some of them are friendly with me. J. M. is trying hard to get me in trouble in the cottage, but I'm ignoring her."

When I asked her, after twenty interviews, whether she still wanted to come twice a week she answered, "In the beginning, when I started talking with you, I didn't know if I was coming or going. I'm better now, so I can come once a week." I reinforced her feelings by pointing to her growth in self-control, to her future as a wife and mother, and her eyes opened wide and her face became flushed when I said, "I'm proud of you, Grace."

During the last few interviews Grace showed poise and self-confidence. In the last interview she reported that even Mrs. N., a hard-to-please cottage counselor, had praised her for her improvement. "I don't listen to the other girls, but I don't quarrel with them either. Only B. G. makes me mad. She's just like I used to be. I felt that everyone was going to crush me, to push me around, and I was putting up a fight. It was foolish."

"What changed it?"

"I used to come here, and you didn't laugh at me. There was someone who understood me, and I slowly changed. Now I am not ashamed of myself. I used to think that even my mom and dad didn't like me because I was bad. But now I'm proud of myself. I'm going to finish school and get a job and stay with mom and dad to make it up to them. I hurt them enough."

"How about Paul?"

"Mother says he's going to the dogs, drinking too much. I knew a good boy. He liked me, but I did not care for him; he was goody-goody. I'll be seeing him when I go home."

Although Grace was yearning to go back to her parents and prove that she was "reformed," as she put it, she accepted without opposition the parole plan to go to a workhome for a few months before being returned to her parents. Along with her childish dependency, she had apparently overcome the intense bitterness against work placement she had exhibited in the beginning of therapy.

In summary, Grace had made great progress from being a capricious, willful child toward becoming an average teen-ager with self-control and a mature handling of stresses. She had relinquished her delinquent pattern to become a responsible, somewhat compulsively proper young lady.

She did well in the workhome, was returned to her parents, and appeared to be adjusting well in the family and in the community.

Test Changes

MMPI: L (63-76), F 73-62, D 61-46, Hy 68-54, Pd 95-57, Mf
    63-51, Pa 100-56, Pt 89-60, Sc 74-57, Ma 75-60, At 36-24,
    Es 31-36, De 34-24, Jh 25-13, Ad 16-22, So-r (23-31)
16PF: C 3-8, G 4-8, M 8-5, N 5-2, Q1 4-7, Q2 (5-2), Q3 3-8
HGI: Ho 38-28, A 8-4, C 6-3
HOW: Tr 96-67, Cr (100-101)

The test changes give the impression that Grace had undergone a definite modification of character. Her animosity to persons in her environment was brought within normal bounds, and her disregard of social controls seems to have disappeared. From a severely hostile, spiteful, and uncooperative young woman she had become a compliant and properly behaving individual. Her hostility, anxiety, and childish demandingness were no longer inappropriately strong. She became more feminine and realistic in her strivings, more conscientious and practical, and is not likely to use subterfuge to gain her ends. Capable of more mature effort toward realistic goals, she may even have become more properly sociable.

Hanna

Age 16, 29 interviews in seven months. I saw her after she had been in the institution about two months because the initial MMPI indicated a severely disturbed individual. She appeared to be a latent schizophrenic, as further observation and clinical impressions later confirmed. She was described by counselors and teachers as "scatter-brained" and a "compulsive talker, often making no sense." She was committed for sexual promiscuity. The judge suggested that she have "psychiatric treatment."

Hanna came from a highly disturbed background. The family had come to Colorado from a southern state. Her father was an unstable worker, losing jobs because of drinking and bad temper. Both parents had impaired hearts. Mother had had several operations for a tumor, gall-stones, et cetera. She was high-strung, Hanna said. There were five children younger than Hanna, the last two being baby twins.

Hanna welcomed the opportunity to talk with me. "I can't talk with my dad. He always flares into a temper. I can't talk with my mother either because she gets easily upset. But I lie in my bed and worry about my family: Is dad working? Is he drinking his paycheck? Did mother divorce him as she threatened? Would the work with the five-month-old twins harm her health again? They never write to me. I mean, they seldom do. I hate my dad for the way he treated the family. He beat mother many times. Once he tried to kill her. I pushed his gun away. Mother ran out and called the police. Father was fined two hundred dollars and put on proba-

73

tion for six months. Father cried when mother ran out that time. I imagined he was ashamed.

"Father hit my brother over the head when he was two years old, and he doesn't hear well now. He's six now, but he talks only when Father isn't there. What's worse, I may be taking after my father. I started drinking, and have an awful temper like him. I used to hit my mother. Once my father knocked me down on the floor when he hit me. I ran away from home, like my father did when he was young. Grampa had a temper like my father. Father tried to kill himself. I wonder if I might not do that sometimes."
She was obviously anxiety-ridden, for good reasons.

In the second interview she related her disappointment with the visit of her parents. They had to drive several hours to the institution, yet they stayed only one hour although they could have stayed longer. Father became fidgety, told her after half an hour: "I think I'd better go out and get ready for that drive back." My feelings were mixed.

Thinking I could feign naiveté with her I asked. "Why?"

"Because I used to cause quarrels between the two of them. One of them would tell me something, and I'd go and tell the other. Dad would get very mad."

Her mother had asked her if she were getting "psychiatric" help. "I told her that I had just begun. She said she'll see how I look in five months."

I asked, "What kind of help do you feel you need?"

"With my temper. The girls annoy me so much. And then I'm so forgetful. I forget where I left my gloves. I forget what I should do. If I didn't have my head fastened to my shoulders I'd forget it somewhere. Then, with my emotions, I get upset so easily, I can't control my feelings. I go to pieces over little things. And then sex. Why do I do it? When I look at a guy a certain way . . . it happens."

I pretended to ignore the long look she directed at me.

Hanna had considerable capacity for insight about her reactions. What she lacked was the ability to integrate insights into her behavior. Her ego was quite ineffective even in areas in which she had some understanding. She apparently lacked models on which to build a socialized personality pattern for herself. She remembered distinctly that when she was three or four years old her mother was in bed with another man, not Hanna's father.

74

She wanted to tell Dad, but was afraid he would kill both her mother and herself. Anyway, she knew without doubt that last year she had seen her mother parked on a side road with Hanna's former boy friend. She also remembered sleeping with her parents when she was quite small, and having them carry on intercourse without interrupting their gossip about Hanna's aunt. As I prompted her toward a catharsis, she wept bitterly with disgust at her father, telling how she found him in a tavern where mother had sent her for him. Both he and the "redhead" were drunk, and he was rubbing her buttocks with one hand and handling her breasts with the other.

Apparently all Hanna learned during the first sixteen years of her life was that people live their impulses without inhibition. She thought of herself as oversexed. A more correct description would have been "undercontrolled." She had had her first sexual experience when she was thirteen years old with a married man of forty, the father of three. Her next experiences were also with older, married men. Prior to commitment she had been "raped" by four fellows, although her leisurely description of that night did not indicate any violent struggle on her part. An uninhibited sexuality had become an avenue of relief from dismal living conditions and the attendant anxieties; it was a way of becoming "someone," of being "superior" to other "nice girls."

She told of feeling, "cheap" if her partner showed no interest in her after sexual intercourse. "My blood would curl [her expression] when I found he did not love me and only wanted sex. Why did I pick on older married men?" she asked looking up straight at me. I led her to talk about her father. "He was always cross with us. Only when he was drunk he'd make me sit on his lap and tell me, 'I love you.' I felt awful. If he really loved me and the others he wouldn't drink. And he didn't have to get drunk to tell me he loved me."

"Does your missing love from your father have something to do with what you asked me?"

Her insight was direct: "Probably . . . I wanted sex because Dad didn't give me love. . . . They never told me anything while I was growing up." I asked if she wanted to read *A Girl Grows Up*. "Yes, that's just down my line."

In that book she discovered that one of the faults of young girls is to disparage themselves. She did not know the meaning of the word, and asked a cottage counselor. Then she used it to make sense of some of her feelings. She told me how she had been left behind one day while other girls were taken to the gym for skating. She became angry, desperate. She took off her belt and tried to choke herself. Then she had remembered that she was unduly "disparaging" herself by feeling they didn't care for her because they hadn't taken her to play, forgetting that she had "a heavy flow" that day.

On another occasion she spoke of blaming herself for getting into fights with girls. "J. pinched me yesterday, and I pinched her back, and we started fighting till M. separated us. In the evening I was so mixed up that I couldn't eat. I couldn't laugh or cry. Then I remembered that I shouldn't disparage myself. I guess that's the same when I blame myself for those guys going to jail for having sex with me because I was under age. They were older. It wasn't my fault."

On many other occasions, however, she was unable to put things together rationally. She confided to me her worry that she was pregnant from her last intercourses. I asked about her periods. She had had them in the last two months. "But my mother was pregnant with my brother and had periods."

"That's rather unlikely."

"But she had a tumor."

"Do you have a tumor?"

"No, I don't . . . oh, I see, Thanks, it's a relief to know I'm not pregnant."

Although possessing average intellectual ability, she appeared like an eight to ten-year-old in her behavior responses. Not only was she forgetful and excitable but was also socially retarded, without poise, decisiveness, or assertiveness. The other girls had noticed her childishness and lack of courage and used her as a scapegoat for their aggressions—as young people often do with odd, defenseless individuals. She seemed to be masochistically oriented so that she provoked their aggressiveness.

Her attempt to escape from the institution was characteristically ineffectual. She did not even leave the school grounds. She described the occasion later: "I ran to the road, I was short of breath and wished to be back in the cottage. I wondered where my meal would come from, where I would sleep. Luckily Mr. S. came by, and I put my arms around him and asked him to take me back.

They didn't punish me like I expected. Mrs. A. told me to think before doing anything next time. I don't think I'll try it again."

Her dependency needs were partly gratified by the pity others felt for her. She told the matron after the first interview that I had shed tears over her story. In a number of interviews she seemed to be genuinely worried about the beatings she anticipated from some Spanish girls. There was a thrill of expectation in her worries, too.

In the face of such massive personality misdevelopment I tried to achieve limited goals only: to help her regain self-respect and a measure of confidence; to lead her to a more balanced perspective of sex in human life; and to encourage her to have a more hopeful and realistic plan for the future. I supported her interest in school subjects, treated her respectfully, emphasizing that the past was past and that what was important was how she handled her sexual urge in the future. I tried to teach her how to control her anger without either being carried away with it or denying it and retreating in fear.

She often promised that she would not be nasty to other girls so that they would like her a little more. I led her to consider that it would be better for her not to return to her sordid family circumstances but to go to a workhome from which she could also go to school. She was so eager to accept advice and be led that she rebuked me one day for not telling her of her worst characteristic. It had been a revelation to Hanna when a cottage counselor told her: "You are refusing to grow, you want ta stay babyish." Hanna thought I should have told her that earlier.

Her progress toward appropriate responses was slow and interspersed with many failures yet she was intent on utilizing my help. One day, she said, "I want you to see me when I'm mad so you can help me better, but then it's not my day for seeing you. Then I start thinking what you would say, and I calm myself down. I think you're helping me, maybe." She proposed that instead of having set interviews she would rather let me know when she needed them.

Many of her "lessons" in the interviews had to be of a concrete nature, as with a child. One day she said she was apprehensive that I might tell the cottage counselors what we talked about. "Some girls say so."

"You've been with me four months. How did I hurt you?"

"You don't." She spoke about something else. I kept silent deliberately. She grew uneasy and asked: "Are you now angry with me?"

I laughed. "No, but I wanted to teach you not to believe your fearful thoughts—not to follow your imagination. You bothered yourself for nothing, thinking I was angry. I was only keeping quiet."

On another occasion she was restless with an unrealistic desire to go to the wedding of her cousin, 350 smiles from the institution. I asked her how she planned to travel. She wanted the head counselor and the superintendent to go with her because she would feel safer that way. I drew a sketch of Colorado for her, showing the far corner where the wedding would take place. "If it is that far, I better give up on it." She did not appear upset at the disillusionment but remained bland and dull.

For a while she was seriously grieved by not having had a visit from her parents for more than five months. "My dad has money for beer, but not for gas to bring the family here." Later she accepted their poverty as a genuine reason for their not visiting her. There was a possibility that the institution might send her home on a bus for a visit. The plan was not approved, and I told her about it. I was surprised at her reasonableness. "Maybe it's better that way. I might get upset, seeing them at home." She also spoke about how now she wanted to be respectable, for she had been known as a bad girl in her small hometown. Apparently feelings of shame and a yearning for a respectable role in life were stirring within her.

The desire to be socially compliant remained shallow and precarious in Hanna. However, the institution could not provide realistic occasions for testing the genuineness of her orientation. I tried to get her asigned to kitchen work, where she could try her willingness to carry on some regular responsibilities. The cottage staff, fearing that she was still scatterbrained and untidy, could not see her as one of the assistant cooks. As a result a stalemate was reached in her progress, even though she was apparently doing well in the classroom and in her limited duties in the cottage.

I felt that I could not help her much more, for it became apparent that the institutional atmosphere, with all its controls, did not provide sufficient testing ground for maturing the self-directiveness of some delinquent youngsters. There was the need for testing Hanna's new reactions in the community, where temptations and pressures toward misbehavior would be greater. It could be said that therapy was only begun for her.

Test Changes

MMPI: *F* 95-73, *K* 29-42, *Hs* (48-68), *Pd* (60-78), *Pt* (66-78), *Ma* 83-73, *At* 36-24, *Es* 31-36, *R* (7-13), *De* 43-34, *Ho* 41-35
16PF: *G* (10-5), *L* 8-5, *M* 8-2, *O* 8-5, *Q3* (4-8), *Q4* 9-6
HGI: *Ho* 50-40, *C* 10-5, *E* (3-7), *G* 11-4, *H* 9-6
HOW: *Tr* 124-111, *Cr* 111-91

In some respects there had been a noticeable deterioration in Hanna's condition. She was less conforming, more preoccupied with her physical states, and compulsively rigid in some of her attitudes. To what extent this was due to strict supervision in the cottage and to the disturbing effects of therapy cannot be determined from data at hand. However, she became less agitated and confused; her capacity to handle the reality of a situation was somewhat improved; and her regression toward childish dependency was less deep. Also, she was less tense and anxious, although her resentment toward her situation grew. She was not so self-depreciating as before therapy; less openly aggressive and suspicious; and her mind was not so often misled by unfriendly or fearful imaginings. Her ability to exercise healthy repression had increased so that she could act somewhat more adaptively.

Judy

Age 13, dull normal IQ, 19 interviews in three months. Judy was committed for repeated running away from home and foster homes. She wrote two notes asking me for an interview. One of the notes read: "I would like very much to talk to you. I would like to talk to you about getting along with some of these girls. And about doing some things that I should not."

I was intensely moved by the emotional plight of this youngster. Her whole body was quivering as she cried bitterly in dejection and fear. She could not get along with people. She thought that her trouble started with her mother, who had left Judy and her older sister alone at home while she went out drinking. Judy knew that other mothers were home with their children. Sometimes she would run away from home, not wanting to be there any more. She felt that her mother showed her partiality to the older sister by handing down the sister's clothing to her. A social worker had placed Judy in two foster homes, but she would not stay in them and wanted to be back with her family.

Here at school Judy felt that the girls talked about her behind her back saying that she was ugly and other "nasty things." She seemed unable to please anyone with her work, although she wanted to be trusted with doing things in the cottage. A girl who stared at her during mealtimes drove Judy frantic; she felt confused when people looked at her. She dreaded the return of the senior counselor from vacation because she didn't trust Judy. Judy wanted to change cottages. She had felt so good at the hospital where just seeing Mrs. Y.'s face had seemed to be enough to keep her out of trouble.

I asked her where she felt most unhappy. She ranked her own home first, then the foster home, and last the institution. "I'm trying to keep out of trouble. I asked Mrs. A. to let me eat in my room, and she did." I persuaded her to try to eat in the dining room with the other girls, just for a day. I offered to see her the next day if she wished. "I wish I could talk with you the whole day about my troubles," she said as she left, sobbing quietly.

The following day she did not look so unhappy, and reported that she had eaten at the table without feeling upset. She showed me a letter she had received from her mother. Its tone was tender and warm. However, Judy felt that it might be better if she went to a foster home instead of back to her mother. "It's better for me to have a Dad. It'd settle me faster when I start doing what I shouldn't."

In the following interview she appeared agitated, clasping her hands, repressing sighs, and avoided talking about her feelings by switching to inconsequential matters. I commented on her worried expression.

"It's about home," she said. She remembered how she had gone to her mother's bed when she felt scared, although her mother had slept just across the room. Even in the daytime, when her mother had been reading, Judy would enjoy lying on her mother's arm

80

and falling asleep. She couldn't bring herself to think that she wouldn't be going back to her mother when she left the institution. Maybe her mother had stopped drinking, as she once had said she would after she hurt her leg in a fall when leaving a tavern. Perhaps she could at least go to her sister. She would be with someone who was close to her. "And my brother-in-law is strict—it's good for me."

In the subsequent interview she reported the return of the senior counselor whom she had dreaded ten days earlier. "We were all glad that Mrs. S. was back. We all wanted to hug her, but two girls got hold of her and wouldn't let go. [Tears] But I'm still scared of her. I wanted to ask her if I could get some of my pictures from the office, but didn't dare to."

"What would she do to you?"

"Guess nothing."

I urged her to talk with Mrs. S. and told her she was a good-hearted woman, though strict.

Judy was delighted with the new job Mrs. S. gave her (dusting), but wished for more important responsibilities. I pointed out that it would depend on how she performed on this job. Judy was now worrying about the skirt her mother had promised to send for her birthday. Also, she was disappointed that her sister forgot to leave money for her on the last visit so that she could buy that big candy bar in the office.

On her birthday I called her in to give her a card and the "big candy bar." She cried, then asked if she could straighten the books in my cabinet. Next she asked for a cloth to dust the furniture and dusted wholeheartedly during a large part of the following interview too. She asked me what I would like her to make for me in the art class—would my wife like a dolly? Judy would like to make one for her. I suggested that she write to my wife, and she promptly did. In another interview she offered me a candy. She brought a framed picture of angels and proudly hung it up in my office. Apparently I had come to stand for her missing daddy.

I treated her in therapy much as I would my own daughter of the same age. I directed her, encouraged or advised against certain behavior, cheered her up when she was gloomy, or chatted about her concerns. She often began the interview by asking if there were something she could do for me, and I usually answered that I appreciated her friendliness but that we had better talk about her.

81

She often avoided just that. She explained her insistence on doing things: "I'll keep asking you till you see that I'm not too young." She asked to do a book report for me; quite a novelty for her, for she only tolerated schoolwork as a necessary evil.

Judy was quite upset after her mother's visit and wanted to go home immediately to help with washing, et cetera. "She's good now. Takes only soft drinks. She promised to go to church with me. She's so skinny now, tinier than I am. She needs me."

On Judy's insistence I let her help an older girl, R., check score columns on adding-machine tapes. R. complained that Judy was not much help because she was too playful. Judy could not keep up with the conscientious effort of R. One morning Judy left the workroom crying, but after an hour or two she returned. I spoke with her. Apparently she had found R. too "bossy," like her older sister. However, Judy had decided to fight against the disturbing memories. "Boy, doesn't R. have a temper! But I have to get along with people, like you told me, even if they are hard to get along with."

When I told her that she would be going home soon, she could hardly contain herself. "Boy, this is the happiest day of my life for me. I was hoping for it ever since I came here."

The following day, before leaving, Judy left for me a page she had torn from a magazine with a poem about a little girl who had so many questions to ask. The illustration accompanying the poem pictured a man holding a little girl on his knee. She apparently appreciated the psychological nursing I had given her. The counselor told me that Judy had wanted to tell her something before leaving, but that her voice had choked in tears. Probably she was afraid to leave a consistent mother for an inconsistent one.

I had mainly tried to reduce the dread of life in this child. Threatened by loneliness and self-doubt she had found in me protection, warm interest, hope. Without it she might have succumbed to paranoid trends which had been obvious before therapy.

Test Changes

MMPI: *F* 78-62, *Hy* 43-31, *Sc* 73-57, *Ma* 68-43, *At* 35-18, *Dq* 14-7, *Jh* 28-14, *Ho,* 36-26, *Ad* 21-30, *So-r* (14-20)
16PF: *B* (6-1), *H* 3-7, *Q2* (1-5)
HGI: *Ho* 42-22, *A* 5-2, *B* 4-1, *C* 9-5, *D* 5-1, *G* 6-3
HOW: *Tr* 84-67, *Cr* 115.5-89

Excitability and emotionalism definitely shrunk to normal limits within Judy. Her response to environment was more appropriate, her fears and hostilities less intense. As she lost her apprehensiveness, she began to come out of her shell. Teachers and counselors alike observed a marked reduction of maladjustment in her.

Kate

Age 16, IQ normal, 25 interviews in five months.

Kate was committed for incorrigibility, drinking and associating with undesirable older girls. The police alleged sexual promiscuity or prostitution, but Kate denied it vigorously. While she had been on probation, the judge allowed her to marry an unstable young soldier. The marriage held for a few months. After its breakdown Kate became unruly in the community and was sent to the institution.

She was referred to me for evaluation and help because the cottage counselors felt they were making no headway with her after three months of training. She was not openly rebellious, but seemed unable to follow instructions, "flighty and scatterbrained." She gave this impression in the first interview: she stared into space, forgetting what she had been talking about; or talked in a fast and indistinct fashion. She was apparently highly anxious, but trying to keep her agitation under control. There was something incongruous about her. Her reactions were those of a child, although the impression was contradicted by her big frame and heavy body. After the interview she ran excitedly along the concrete walk like a grade school girl delighted with her talk with the principal.

She complained of her bad temper, quarreled with girls too much, said bad words. I wanted to test her feelings of shame and asked: "What do you say to them?"

She didn't want to pronounce them in front of me. "I use them only when I'm mad." She wondered if she were crazy because she had "such wild daydreams." She wanted to finish school and be an office worker. "It was foolish to get married at fifteen. I'm still Momie's baby, and he's still Momie's boy."

She alternated between states of agitation and calm in almost every interview. When agitated, she expressed anger against institutional controls. She was afraid that she would blow up any

83

time. "This happened every two or three months when I was home." She complained about the coldness and strictness of the counselors, comparing them unfavorably with the friendly nuns in an orphanage where she had spent several years after her dad had died in an accident. She would be overcome by her wish to be back with her mom. "I wonder if they'd let me out sooner if I misbehaved badly in the cottage." I explained that any uncontrolled behavior would be interpreted as a sign that she was still unstable and would keep her longer in the institution. She nodded, apparently giving up a pet scheme.

Kate had answered an "officer" rudely, and was confined to her room for a few days. She was apparently touched by my coming over to the cottage to talk with her. She vowed in the beginning of the interview that she was not going to apologize to that "officer," then promised spontaneously at the end of the hour that she would do just that. She accepted my suggestion that it would be better for her to use the punishment time to study shorthand than to fret and fume against the unavoidable.

Her restlessness was not deep-seated. Sometimes she overplayed it in order to enjoy my concern and to hear sensible considerations. It helped her to know that I regarded her resentment against the institution as natural but childish. "I hate this place," she would say. "I wish I were back in jail. I'll ask Miss P. to send me back. . . . Would they send me to the hospital at Pueblo? I'm sure it'd be better than this place. How can I get out of here?"

I replied with variations of: "You can get out of here when you show you can control your wild notions. You are unhappy; that's why thoughts are racing through your head. But let's think out now what would be best for you in the long run." She would then soon become quieted and rational.

Although she rebelled against a strict cottage counselor, Kate appeared genuinely sad and afraid when the woman had been overheard saying that she was going to leave because she had had enough headaches with "these stubborn girls." Kate's feeling about the institution remained ambivalent, but her disgust with "this damn place" weakened. Her mood swings were less extreme, and she was surprised at the quiet she experienced within herself. "The other day I felt my old mad self, and I felt funny. It was foolish to be that way. I feel better when I am quiet."

She had periods of cheerfulness without exuberance, also she proudly reported that she was now trying to think before acting. "The other day I apologized to Mrs. C. for telling her the day before that I hated her. This morning a girl made me mad, and I wasn't going to go to work in the kitchen. But then I changed my mind because I thought they might not let me go out when Mom comes."

"How would you have handled it before?"

"I would have rushed into it without thinking."

The progress towards rational self-direction was neither fast nor uninterrupted. Sometimes Kate despaired of ever becoming satisfactory to the counselors, for they would reproach her for singing in the bath or munching carrots or having untidy hair. She wished she could be a "regular girl." When I asked her to explain she said: "I've learned quite a number of useful things here. I can work better now. But I should have learned those things at home. I didn't need to come here to waste a year. And I did some bad things. Also got married too young. I wish I'd never had to go to that orphanage after my dad died in that accident. Then Mother got married. My stepfather hated me and beat me. I'm sorry now for that man. He must have been very unhappy to drink that much and do what he did to me. Mother left him, and got married again before I came here. I didn't want to listen to my new stepfather. I wanted only pleasures and independence, but no responsibility. Why do I have to learn it the hard way, when other girls never get in these troubles?"

I reinforced her orientation toward future opportunities away from the failures of the past. She remarked that she had "learned how to worry" only two months ago. Before she hadn't cared what happened. Now she was often afraid about what some of the "the officers" might think of her and became upset when she thought they didn't like her. She was also afraid of how things would turn out after she left. She had never before given a serious thought to such matters; obviously she was relinquishing the shortsighted perspective so characterictic of delinquent, impulse-ridden individuals.

When our relationship had solidified I informed Kate that counselors and teachers thought she had not yet improved enough, that she talked too much and was inattentive. She refused at first to examine the reasons for her excessive talking, but later yielded to my pressure to look behind her actions. She came up with the explanation that she couldn't hold her tongue because of her un-happiness about being away from her mother and feeling that she was a bad girl. Talking helped cover up these sad feelings. "That's why I like to come here. I can tell of all my hatred of this place, and you wouldn't rat me off."

It was apparent that she had become emotionally dependent on our interviews. One day I couldn't see her at the regular time. The following day she reported her reaction. "When you didn't call me, I felt so sorry for myself I didn't want to do any work in the kitchen. I've got used to our talks, sort of. I feel better afterwards. I asked B., who saw you earlier in the morning, if you were busy and she said yes. Then I didn't feel so bad, and I could work in the kitchen." Obviously, even remote signs of rejection appeared threatening to her.

When I learned that I was going to leave the institution I be-gan to announce it to the girls I had been seeing in therapy. Kate had heard about it through one of these girls before she came to the interview. She tried to be gay. "Oh, you traitor! Leaving us, ha? How are they better over there? Oh, I'm kidding. They may need you over there. But so suddenly . . ." Her voice trailed off.

I explained that the superintendent had agreed that I might continue seeing the girls for about six more weeks, so that I would not leave them abruptly. "I can still talk with you in a number of interviews," I said trying to cheer her up. Apparently, the separation was too hard for her.

She replied: "No, I won't see you. Other girls need you more." As tears came, she got up and went into the corridor. I went after her, called her back in, and told her that I understood her friendly feelings for me. I suggested that she might write me a note if she later wanted to talk with me. She didn't think she would do that. "I'm not so bad off nowadays. I'm behaving better." I understood that her memories of unreliable males in her past were too disrupting for her to handle. She never asked for an interview in the following weeks, but told other girls to say hello to me for her.

In summary, Kate established controls over her hysterical pro-pensities, became less excitable, and began rejecting her childish needs. She experienced the satisfying inner state that comes with more responsible behavior. These memories of effective personality reactions may serve as an important defense when she starts facing pressures and temptations in the community.

Test Changes

MMPI: *Ma* (48-63), *Si* 63-51, *A* 20-13, *At* 19-9, *Cn* 20-25, *De* 29-21, *Do* 14-21, *Ca* 15-10, *Jh* 17-12, *Ho* 25-18, *Ad* 24-31, *Dn* 12-18, *So-r* (26-33)
16PF: *A* 2-6, *L* 6-3, *Q1* 3-6, *Q3* 6-9, *Q4* 6-3
HGI: *Ho* 41-32, *B* (3-6), *C* 9-0, *H* (4-7)
HOW: *Tr* 106-79, *Cr* (89.5-97.5)

Kate had brought within control many of the sources of her agitation: anxiety and aggressiveness, dependency strivings and withdrawing trends, suspiciousness and inability to rely upon herself. She had acquired a measure of self-directiveness that would enable her to cope more consistently with strains of adjustment.

Lou

Age 14, IQ normal, 16 interview in five months.

She was committed for repeatedly running away from home and associating with girls who were known to the police. She was the oldest in a large family. Her father was a laborer. Lou had asked me twice, through another girl, if she could see me before she got into trouble.

In the interview she described her main trouble as wanting to fight with other girls. She did not want to do this because it might prevent her going out with her parents. She explained that she had been "bad" and had hurt her mother, and that she had not listened to what her mother told her. Now she wanted to become good quickly in the institution, so that they would let her go back to her mother to show her that she could be a good girl.

The girls bossed her too much, she felt, and she had decided not to yield an inch; but now she agreed with me that she had to find some other way of handling her angry feelings. She would withdraw to her room when she felt annoyed with the other girls. Instead of fighting when angry, she would walk away even at the risk of being called "chicken." When other girls started getting excited about petty quarrels, Lou would ignore them by telling herself it was none of her business.

The fund of hostility in Lou seemed inexhaustible. When she had successfully managed her rage against the girls in her cottage, she became irritated with girls in the classroom for their bragging. She thought a teacher was picking on her because she disliked all Spanish girls. Against another teacher, who she thought was too grouchy, she conducted a foot-shuffling campaign.

In the fourth interview Lou became uncommunicative. She was feeling fine now; there were no troubles to talk about. To my questions, she replied by whispering "yes," "no," and "I don't know." Apparently, so far as she could see, the interviews had achieved the desired goal. Of course she could not sense that I had another goal—to achieve certain more basic changes than learning to handle hostility by evasion and repression. When several probing attempts failed to move her from complacency I asked whether she wanted to come once or twice a week. After a lot of hesitation, she whispered; "Once, I guess, as I'm no more upset."

Most of the remaining interviews showed the same taciturn, resistive pattern. She usually began by whispering "things are fine now," and sat with her head low and shuffled her feet on the floor. My questioning usually uncovered some annoyance or worry that some girl might get her into trouble by making her mad, yet she soon repressed the intimations of turbulence by statements about how she was able to hold her temper.

She was not trying to annoy the teachers any more. Now she could do what she was told. She asserted a new interest in school subjects, though she had once been "so bored by the teacher's voice" that she could not stay in school. She would say, as if trying to convince herself, "I know now that I should obey for my own good. I should have learned that lesson at home instead of doing what I wanted and against orders. I was just running away from things, and that solves nothing."

I often coached her directly in ways of handling tense situations with some of the girls and counselors. Usually she didn't dare apply the technique but reported in the subsequent interview that the problem had settled itself. Feeling that I was not helping her, I asked if she would like to discontinue her regular visits and come only when she felt the need of discussing things with me. She wanted to keep regular appointments. "It helps me to think more clearly because, when I get problems, I don't know

88

how to start solving them." Apparently her excitement and hostility were interfering with her reasoning, and the contact with me enabled her to keep her impulse in check; or maybe Lou was changing without being aware of it, like two of Morse's (1958) patients who achieved no insight and yet reached some desirable changes through identification with the therapist and introjection of his standards.

In the last interview she reported that she was working in the kitchen, that she didn't like the dietician but kept out of her way and did her part of the work. Nothing bothered her, and everything was "fine" as usual. The cottage counselor did not quite agree with this evaluation but she had given up on pressing Lou further. She felt helpless, as did I, in efforts to change Lou. However, she had progressed in socializing her hostile feelings and managing them by repression like most "normal" individuals. This might have been an important gain for a deeply angry and negativistic adolescent.

Test Changes

MMPI: *Ma* (50-63), *Si* 55-44, *A* 14-9, *Rec* (7-12)
16PF: *C* 6-9, *Q3* (8-4)
HGI: *Ho* 44-39
HOW: *Tr* (63-80), *Cr* 117.5-103

Lou had toned down her intense hostility. Her withdrawal trends were less pronounced, and her anxiety had lessened somewhat. Possibly less compulsive about her work, she may also lack enough will power to carry her through successful adaptation. Her reality testing is better.

Mary

Age 17, IQ normal, 20 interviews in three months.

Committed for leaving parental home, then fighting two policemen who came to arrest her after she had refused to obey her probation officer. She was referred to me by the nurse, who was concerned by her loss of weight, her consistently low mood and possible suicidal trends.

Mary was ambivalent about starting interviews. She was quite tense, laughing nervously in contrast with her dignified and cold mien. In the beginning of the interview she said she felt fine. Later she broke through her reserve with a genuine expression: "I'd like to know what made me do these things, like running away. But I'm also afraid to learn about it." She decided she would try interviews for three months.

At the beginning of every interview, even toward the end of the series, I had to ease her apprehensiveness and guardedness. She said she didn't trust anyone, neither girls nor grown-ups. Other girls used to say that she was stuck-up. She explained that she was not, but simply had tried to be ladylike and tidy in her dress. She had taken a modeling course, and didn't want to be slovenly like the girls in her neighborhood.

As the interview progressed, she became more able to consider her feelings spontaneously. She expressed dislike of her excitability and nervousness. "A year ago I understood that I was laughing because I was tense. Someone told me that I must be always happy because I was laughing, and I wasn't happy at all." This was obvious. She was one of the most consistently depressed girls I have met in the institution. Her unhappiness was not of the impulsive, aggressive type; it was quiet, deep, and confirmed.

She remembered that even in fourth grade she had been unhappy over many things. Her father had beaten her mother; her mother had taken it quietly, without protest. Mary had always been fearful of her dad. He was uneasy around her too. When she brought home *B*'s on her report card and thought that she had done well, dad was not satisfied because they were not *A*'s. "I often wondered if he really was my father, though I know he was. He often said harsh things to us and later said he didn't mean them, but it was no use because it had hurt already." She became fearful and refused to do exams, even in grade school. "I was scared of not knowing the answer."

The only bright spot in this dark and fearful atmosphere of her childhood was her grandpa, who used to take her places and buy her things. Then he had suddenly died, and the bottom fell out of her world. She felt that anyone whom she might get to love might die. She loved her older brother. He was intelligent, and they had been real buddies. When he left for military service, she again felt the way she had when her grandfather died. "I couldn't stay in my home. I had to leave." There was a definite compulsive component in her.

90

In grade school she began fighting with girls, and even with boys; she would pick fights with several girls in a group. She was expelled from Junior High for fighting and was sent to G.S. (home for predelinquent girls). When they let her go home, Mary refused to go to school. It hurt her deeply that her father rebuked her younger sisters by saying that they would "turn out like Mary" and end up in a institution.

One evening, when she was fourteen, she had been walking past a local park, as she often did, absorbed in her thoughts, when two young fellows grabbed her and pulled her into the park. One of them raped her while the other held her. Two friends of her brother's came that way by chance and rescued her. When she saw them, she fainted. They carried her to the home of one of the boys, and his mother comforted her. Later this boy was killed in a gang fight, and Mary mourned him as if he had been her brother. It was yet another confirmation that those she loved would perish and leave her with sorrow.

After four interviews Mary learned that her grandmother had died. She was allowed to attend the funeral. Her agitation was intensified by the experience. She escaped, but was returned to the institution two months later. She refused to eat, and I was called on the case again.

She said quietly, "I hate this place and won't take anything from it." She did not appear impressed by my arguments about spoiled health and beauty, but her resistance was not as adamant as it had been in the beginning. In an interview two days later she repeated that she had tried to eat, but food "tasted rotten." I repeated seriously and emphatically: "It tastes rotten." She giggled at this. Apparently her depression was lifting.

I arranged with the parole agent that Mary be assured that her parents could visit her before Christmas. I also told her of a telephone call I had made to her mother, and Mary seemed to become less reserved. She wanted a candy bar, and I sent her one after the interview. Her more relaxed attitude in interviews indicated that I had partly succeeded in correcting her impression of older males as being like her father: depriving and rejecting.

As she relaxed her secretiveness she was able to speak of her disturbed relationships with young males. She used her boy friends as targets for her accumulated hostility, particularly when they tried to be amorous. She couldn't stand their closeness, al-

91

though at the same time she fostered it. Being quite attractive and deliberately vindictive toward males, she provoked some of them to a state of frenzy. One of them, in his frustration, had pulled a knife to kill her. She had spitefully moved closer to him, urging him coldly to stab her. He had turned away in fear, saying only, "You're crazy."

Mary felt herself incapable of loving or trusting any man, though she agreed with me that the rape had colored her attitude toward men in the wrong way.

"Are you afraid of me too?" I asked her, in about the fifteenth interview.

"Still a little," she replied, watching my face intently, at the same time smiling coyly and defiantly.

"Do I make you angry?" I asked further, possibly projecting my own reaction upon her.

"No, because I know it's not your fault. It's my own feelings, my moods, that make me unhappy. You are trying to help."

"My questions sometimes seem to bother you."

"Any questions bother me. The world bothers me. I was never happy." She had an outbreak of anxiety after being returned to the institution. In the night, in dreams, she saw her grandma talking to her tenderly. These appearances occurred in daydreams too. Grandma appeared to her just as she had looked on her last visit to Mary in the institution, a week before her death. Mary could not translate for me the endearing words—her grandmother spoke to her in Spanish—but she conveyed her feeling that it was like the old days when she had been a small girl and her Grandma took care of her.

After these hallucinations Mary cried, wishing her grandmother were with her. She was also oppressed by a feeling of boredom. Reality was apparently blurred and mixed with dreamy experiences so that her fears had full sway. It seemed to her that in her dreams she had gone through phases of her life which later actually had occurred exactly as she had foreseen them: being in the institution, escaping, finding mother sick, the events that took place after she returned to the institution. . . . "That's why everything tires me so much. I've seen my mother die in my dreams, and she is going to die, like grandma did. My thoughts are always sad. The girl's mother died in this book I am reading, and I know mine will too. I always think bad, disappointing thoughts so that I won't get disappointed later."

I led her to recognize that much of her hatred and fear was connected with experiences with her father. This insight did not lead to an appreciable change in mood. See began the subsequent interview by stating that her depression was still the same. "I still hate this place, everything in it. I know they're trying to help me, but I don't like that because I don't want to feel warm toward anyone here. I don't care for anyone except my family. Everyone else is like furniture, like wood, to me. I started fighting everyone when I was eight. I went on with it for four years, and they thought of sending me to this institution then. But I changed my attitude, I spoke with some of the kids. I saw I could not fight the whole world. I hit the matron in Juvenile Hall, and two men had to come in to take me off her. I would have killed her. . . . Later I thought she wasn't worth it. You suffer in prison all your life."

"Do you want to be warmer toward other people, or are you comfortable in your frozen attitude toward them?"

"Sometimes I want to be different, but it's no use anyway; they don't like you; they're two-faced. I don't trust them."

"Me too?"

"Yes, sometimes."

"Do you feel sometimes like hitting me over the head?"

"Yes. But it's not your fault. It's me, because I want to be left alone. But I also like to talk with you. It helps me."

In order to undercut her suspiciousness by pointing to her freedom to use psychotherapy or refuse it, and to gauge her interest in therapy, I often asked her whether she wanted to talk with me next time. Usually she was noncommittal, saying: "It's up to you."

"No, it's your hour. You can have it or not have it."

"I don't care. Guys used to get mad at me when I wouldn't say. I was always teasing them that way."

"I'll do as you say."

"Then I'll see you."

Mary showed considerable interest in the idea of happiness which I suggested to her. She was scornful about the possibility of happiness because there seemed to be nothing to live for. All the pleasures she had had in the past left her with a hollow feeling. I praised her depth of feeling, compared it with those sages of the past who had sought happiness and found it only in a loving and helpful attitude toward people about them. I mentioned that I would be willing to lend her some books on the subject; she eagerly asked for them. She read and asked questions, but soon neglected reading.

As the time of termination of my contact with her approached, she became more agitated in her rejection of the institution. "Mr. T. left. Now you're leaving too. Except Mrs. Y., who's left in this crummy place?" I tried to turn her attention to others whom she might find kind if she got to know them; I also stressed the forms of behavior, that would be in her best interest. She repeatedly threatened to run away. I tried to counteract her impulsiveness by considerations of her long-term future, her need to demonstrate to her worried parents and the Parole Board that she had matured.

Four months after the last interview she was still in the institution, adjusting in an outwardly satisfactory fashion, and being considered for parole. Her parents contacted me to ask whether I would take her as my private patient because they were worried about what might happen on her return home. They said that I was the only man she was willing to talk with for psychological help.

If psychotherapy is thought of as inducing changes in a maladjusted personality pattern, then psychotherapy had only begun for Mary. She had come to see that she was creating her own unhappiness, and she was making sluggish moves toward avoiding disturbing trends. Perhaps her greatest gain had been in experiencing the comfort of a friendly relationship with a professional helper; this might encourage her to seek further help when she became troubled in later stages of her life.

Test Changes

MMPI: F 90-73, K 46-57, Pa 79-65, Si 89-77, Ma 86-73, Dq
    22-15, Jh 29-19, Ho 33-20
16PF: G 4-8, Q1 4-8
HGI: —
HOW: Tr (63-90), Cr (72-78)

Considering Mary's long-standing conflicts with persons in her environment, the reduction of her paranoid trends, and of her intense tendencies towards withdrawal can be considered signs of definite success in therapy. She became less excitable, less hostile, and less rigid in her approach to reality. Her emotional and social maturity had improved, and her delinquent trends diminished. The observers had not yet come to see any improvement in the cold and aloof person she presented to them. Her school phobia is reflected in teacher's ratings.

Nora

Age 17, IQ normal, 15 interviews in three months.

She was commited for incorrigibility and running away from home. Nora asked for an interview on her own.

"A girl told me I better see you. I was putting it off for a week, but can't any more. I don't know what is wrong with me. In the beginning I liked it here. But now I'm getting so snappy. I talked back to Mrs. C. this morning, though I like her. I apologized later. I can't get along with girls."

"What's making you unhappy?"

"Other girls have their parents visit them. My mother doesn't even write. [Her chin was quivering]. She should never have got married. All she cares about is men. She leaves home, going away with them for two or three days. She and dad were fighting something awful. He gave up drinking when she promised to settle, but she didn't. I don't like her as a mother. I love Pat's mother, that's my girl friend, as if she was my mother. She was kinder to me. When I hear Mrs. Z. shout at other girls it upsets me because it reminds me of how mother yelled at me and beat me. . . . I'm worried about Kathy. That's my sister. She's ten now. She begged me not to tell the court what mother was doing, so they wouldn't put her in a foster home. I didn't tell, but now I think it would have been better for my sister if I had told on my mother. Once Kathy had fever, 104 degrees, and mother said it was nothing, just tonsils [angry shudder]. I've always worried a lot. Nothing went right for me."

In the following interview she asked me not to call her by her name because her mother used it. She preferred Ruby instead, as friends called her. She spoke of how unsympathetic her mother had been when her parakeet died, so that Nora had screamed at her in disgust. Once she had pinned down her mother in a pillow fight, and her mother had gotten really mad. Nora thought her mother favored the younger daughter who never criticized her for drinking. In order to spite Nora, her mother had given Nora's clothes to her sister to wear, although Nora bought her own clothes with money earned as a baby-sitter. Nora had tried to get her mother to think of her health because her doctor told her she was digging her own grave.

It seemed to Nora that her mother wanted her to be like her, to drink and go out with men. But Nora never let any man touch her, and she did not drink. Then Nora began presenting a socially desirable picture of herself: how she had been taught at home not to speak back to elders, how she had run away from some guys who intended to rape her, etc.

In subsequent interviews she often presented herself in accordance with her view of the socially appropriate. Her resistances grew stronger in later meetings. She chatted merrily about petty worries, but neglected my promptings to consider her feelings. She often sat sideways, not looking at me. She began the eighth interview red in the face and mumbling something that was later clarified as her not desiring to see me any more. Yet at the end of the interview she wanted to go on with therapy. "It bothers me in the beginning," she explained, "I feel scared. But after talking, I feel better." Probably, I was pushing her to go faster in therapy than was comfortable for her.

While she was in the city hospital for a week for surgery she met a woman whom she grew to like very much, in contrast to her feelings about her mother who had visited her there. Her parents had remarried, and her mother wanted Nora to come home. But Nora was reluctant because her mother's temper might cause trouble again, although both parents said they had stopped drinking. Nora remembered how her mother had thrown dishes at her father or had broken them on the floor. Once she had thrown the telephone at Nora's father. Nora seemed relieved when I explained that her mother had no rights over her now and that the Parole Board would take Nora's desires into account.

In the last few interviews, Nora appeared more agitated and childish than usual. She was annoyed by limits imposed because of her medical condition. She thought her poor cottage grades were unfairly determined, threatened to run away, could not concentrate on schoolwork, was worried about her youngest sister, et cetera. She repeated in two interviews that there was something she didn't want to tell me because I would hate her for it, and refused to respond to my attempts to make her less apprehensive. Finally I realized that she was using this as a teasing game.

In the fifteenth interview she said, in a friendly and nervous way, that she did not want to see me any more. Only after considerable probing did she bring up two "reasons": she had a feeling that I was trying to talk her out of going home, and she hated to be pushed around by anyone; and she also said that she felt she might reveal something to me she would be sorry for later. She explained that she had never trusted people because they had hurt her, and her father and mother had never respected secrets she told them. She thanked me for trying to help her, but it was no use.

I left the institution two weeks later, so there was no opportunity for her to return to therapy as I expected she might have done after a few weeks.

Test Changes

MMPI: Hy 72-57, Pa (62-73), A 26-17, At 30-24, R 24-15,
     So-r (16-22)
16PF: F 4-8, Q4 9-5
HGI: G (7-10)
HOW: Tr 62-59, Cr 90-73

In spite of considerable resistance and interrupted therapy, Nora showed some clear progress in lower anxiety and tension scores. She relinquished her hysterical trends, and affirmed a greater zest for life and activity. Heightened suspiciousness and interpersonal sensitivity, in combination with lowered repressive barriers, may partly explain her interruption of therapy.

Olga

Age 17, low average intelligence, 25 interviews in three months. Committed for running away from home, incorrigibility, sexual promiscuity. She was the only girl brought to the institution with shackles on her wrists, because she and another girl had beaten a matron in Juvenile Hall and tried to snatch her keys.

Olga had asked for an interview on her own. She was afraid of her strong temptation to run away. When she was about thirteen she had talked with a doctor at the city hospital and she had felt good, but had stopped going after a few weeks. "I feel lonesome. I want to be with my folks. I didn't get along with them before, but I know now that they were trying to control me for my own good."

This statement made in the first interview set the pattern for her later relationship with me. I was a substitute for her immature ego, a benevolent controller, a consoling parent. Her emotional instability and domination by fantasy, revealed in initial interviews, were also indicative of her relationship with me throughout therapy. Like Hanna, Olga was a latent schizophrenic. The distinction between reality and fantasy was frequently blurred. Her perception was often distorted by emotional pressures, so that much of her fear and anger was inappropriate and exaggerated. I was not always able to distinguish between her descriptions of real happenings and her imaginative elaborations, but did not feel that I should challenge her.

In one interview she related how she had visited the local Air Force base. She had been sitting with a group of airmen in the club, when one of the airmen had begun to make fun of her "nation," the Indians. She had bent under the table and, pretending to tie her shoe, had bitten him on the calf. "He screamed bloody murder," and had taken her to his officer. The tale seemed typical of the mixture of fantasy and reality in her waking state.

She told of her desire to marry her boy friend, to whom she had been engaged for nine years; but her father had prevented it, and the boy was shipped to Germany when he joined the Armed Forces. Olga had been accused of stealing rings from a home, but she explained this away by attributing it to the manipulations of a girl friend who wanted to get rid of her and marry Olga's boy friend.

She spoke of her last sexual experience as the only one, but was quite evasive. She could not talk clearly about something that happened to her, or else to her father, for which her brother could get the gas chamber because Olga and her brother were close and he would revenge her. "His soul was broken through

98

what happened." The fifteen-year-old brother was in an industrial school at that time. The guilt and loneliness weighed heavily on her. She complained of the dullness of institutional religious services compared with the liveliness of worship in her sect. She thought it was unfair that she was not allowed to wear her hair in braids according to the percepts of her "religion."

I used her religious interests not only to repress her hostility to the institutional pressures but also to decrease her despair and emotionality. She said in an interview: "I wish I was never born."

"How does that fit with your religion?"

"I know I should not feel this way."

"Are you a worse sinner than Mary Magdalene was?"

She smiled quietly, gratefully: "No. . . . Can I come again to speak with you?"

She quickly identified with cultural interests of which she thought I would approve. One day she complained of her fears that she was crazy. The explanation was again a mixture of fantasy and realistic observation. "I'm different from others. I like quiet music. Rock-and-roll makes me sick after two numbers. I like 'sympathies,'—or however you call them. Could listen to them for days. I also like very much western religious music. I get carried away by stories I read. I imagine myself as a princess or a fairy. . . . It's so immature. I should have grown up by now. I like to play baseball with boys while other girls think of clothes and parties. My parents told me that boys were all devils. I guess I wanted to prove that it was not that way, so I got into a number of messes [deep sigh]. . . . My parents considered me a witch. My brother told me that I was born with skin over my face and they had to sew it up. I didn't believe it, but it hurt me. Dad never trusted me fully. He got scared one day when I was playing with some chemicals over fire, and they made flames of many colors. He ran out of the house when I chased him with it. Neither he nor mother trusted me even after I took them to an evangelist—and he preached on the subject of trust. Mother had pains one day, and she said it was because I was evil and had quarreled with her, though the doctors found she had gall-bladder pains. One day she threw me out of the house and said, 'I wish you'd die,' An aunt said one day that she saw a devil with a crown sitting next to me. I've always hated her. I fought them back, but it hurt me, really. I wish they'd trusted me just for a day to show them that I wasn't evil. They didn't, and I went on to prove that I was what they called me."

I tried to strengthen her orientation to realistic, possible tasks and to a less emotional view of both her past and present. I explained the superstitions of her parents by their "Indian" origin and their lack of schooling. I tried to lead her into thinking practically about what she could do with her life. Having felt unloved by the family in comparison with younger siblings, Olga proposed overly ambitious schemes. "You know, you asked me about the future last time, and I said there was no future for me. Later I thought about it, and decided that I want to be a teacher to my people. They were treated brutally by the whites. I want to go as a missionary to them. Even if my parents didn't love me, I can do some good for others. And I want to be good to my parents, even though they hurt me before. If they don't love me, I have God beside me to give me strength."

I encouraged her to take more interest in school subjects. She responded enthusiastically at first, but was soon discouraged by her inability to concentrate consistently. She saw that her worries interfered. She became less severe in her self-reproaches about past "sins." She explained that her sexual misbehavior and drinking were the result of keeping bad company. "I dropped out of church where I had clean fun, real fun. I don't want to go back to bad days. Maybe this place will help me, too, although I still want to be with my family. I'll be going to school, and that will keep me out of trouble, too." She was surprised that she no longer hated the Juvenile Court judge who had sent her to the institution. "If anyone mentioned his name before, ugh! But now I see that he did it for my own good. I'm growing. . . . Tell me what that means."

I reinforced her more mature trends toward a more responsible and practical attitude. However, her progess was far from smooth. Strong anxieties would arise within her, and she would be tempted to use her former method of relief—running away. One day she reported that she had taken a few steps behind the cottage, as if trying to escape, then stopped herself.

"Was it devil or angel?" I asked.

"Angel was stopping me, devil pushing," she answered laughing.

A yearning for the experience of parental love occasionally became very strong, and she would lament that her parents had never understood or wanted her. I pointed out that if her daddy had wanted her to leave him he would not have stopped her early marriage. Her face beamed with the new idea. "Could that be? Oh, Dr. Ray!" she exclaimed in delight. But her hatred of a controlling adult could still be easily aroused.

For a while, she complained bitterly about having to sleep with curlers in her hair. Mrs. Z. had threatened to cut off her hair if she did not take good care of it. Olga shuddered before such a possible catastrophy. She felt that as a short-haired Indian she would be completely dishonored. She relished the fantasy of ruling it over Mrs. Z. just for one day, maltreating her in various ways, even killing her. I pointed out that any disobedience would postpone the day of rejoining her family; with a sigh she promised that she would try to get used to the curlers.

The following time, on the thirteenth interview, she asked me if there were any hidden microphones in the room, for in that case she would not be able to continue talking with me. Apparently she was disappointed with my lack of sympathy for the troubles she was having with the curlers, but this interpretation was not communicated to her because it would have been premature.

On the whole, however, she relaxed some of her suspiciousness of cottage counselors and teachers. "I never thought before that strangers could be your friends and take interest in you like your parents. When I talk with Mrs. R., I feel like I'm talking with my mother." This appeared to be a veiled statement of satisfaction with the therapy situation, just as she was apparently referring to me when she spoke another time about her fear of Mrs. C., whom she also liked; this was during an additional interview which Olga had requested because I had missed seeing her at the regular hour owing to an unexpected obligation. She spoke further of how she used to be seized with fear when she saw certain men and women in the streets, and would run away from them, and at the same time feel embarrassed for being so childish. I sympathized with her strongly ambivalent feelings about people, and pointed out that it was natural to feel confused when we have conflicting feelings until we find ways of reacting to others less emotionally.

I felt comfortable in overtly meeting some of Olga's dependency needs. Before Thanksgiving, for instance, Olga became depressed

101

when remembering past family occasions of mirth and warmth. But on the whole, her early memories were unpleasant. Her parents had not let her play with other children because they said she had a heart condition. She felt they were unfair to her, though she knew they acted in response to the doctor's orders. She cried softly in self-pity during the interview. My tender response to these feelings seemed to satisfy her. Toward the end she was able to relinquish some of her "dark" thoughts, and smilingly accepted my reminder that the sun is in the skies even when clouds temporarily cover it. I felt toward Olga as a nurse might feel toward a physically sick patient, indulging her even in regressive demands.

Olga reported an experience of peace and bliss which puzzled her. "I sat in the window watching the snow all last night." Wanting to keep her close to reality considerations and prevent her efforts at self-harm, which I suspected, I asked her: "What did you put on?"

"Nothing."

"On your feet?"

"I was barefoot. I felt so warm I even opened the window a little. But I felt so good this morning. There was peace inside me. I wasn't sorry that I wasn't with my parents, like I usually am. . . . I feel strange nowadays, like I am living two lives. It seems like I depart to Russia or Germany. My body stays here, and I return to it in the morning. I may sound funny to you, but I am saving some kids from concentration camps and trying to get their parents out. Some other people are helping me. I guess I find these are people who are in much tougher spots than me, and I can take my being here easier. I can see that even what happened in my childhood was part of God's will for me. . . . I wonder if I'm going crazy."

I used this occasion to direct her towards sublimation. "No, you are learning that one way to overcome our troubles is to help others who are in trouble."

Because of the dissociative treads underlying her experiences I offered to see her again the next day. Her eyes glistened as she said, "Yes, Dr. Ray." In the following interview she reported that she again had not slept all night, but had put a blanket over her shoulders and slippers on her feet, "as you told me." She was angry with some of the girls for making fun of Indians, but decided

102

that it was no use getting angry with them because they spoke out of ignorance. "They are stupid like me. If I wasn't stupid, I wouldn't be here now."

"You are not stupid, only you have not used your mind properly."

"I started using my brains the first time in my life when I came here."

Consistent in my didactic role, I disagreed with her proud self appraisal and wondered openly whether this was wishful thinking. She had told me in the same interview that she could not stop herself from giggling at the table; she had asked her mother in a letter to bring her a deer-meat sandwich because she did not like the food cooked in the institution; and she had been involuntarily doing arithmetic problems in a way opposite to that recommended by the teacher. Interestingly enough, her manifest behavior was not severely affected by the apparent internal loosening. I called Olga's cottage counselor, a strict and demanding lady, who reported that Olga was not doing badly.

In the subsequent interview Olga complained that she wished they would give her something to do in her room to keep troublesome thoughts away. The following interview was held sooner than usual at Olga's request. She appeared distressed: "I'm scared of everyone."

"Don't fight those tears."

"I'm an Indian."

"I still think there is no shame in crying." She had again been overcome by memories of old hurts: her aunt had pushed Olga around, and Olga had called her a whore, "And that's what she is, while I am still a virgin"; her grandma had said that Olga would end in a school for "bad girls" because grandma was angry at Olga's parents for removing Olga to their home after she spent years with her grandparents; when Mrs. Z. called other girls stupid, Olga felt that she meant her.

I interpreted:

"No one loves Olga."

"Don't speak like that. I'm going to break down and won't be able to stop crying."

"You'll feel better afterward."

As Olga still appeared disconsolate and seemed to have been

hedging about something disturbing to her, I extended the interview and told her that I felt she was holding back something. Since she couldn't bring herself to speak about it, I suggested she write. She wrote a note, but could hardly hand it across the desk. The note read: "I have fallen in love with you. I am very, very sorry, Dr. Ray. I just don't know what has come over me." She said she was disgusted with herself, would be ashamed to see me in the future. She felt like running away again from the institution. I reassured her that she need not be afraid since I was not going to hurt her. "Did other girls come to feel the same way?"

"Some of them."

"Well, maybe it's not so bad then."

Olga brought her New Testament to the following interview. "I prayed over what we spoke about last night and got it clear. I like you as a father. I could talk to him at home, but here I can't. You're instead of him. It's not that other kind of love. You're my friend."

I explained how our feelings can flow from one type of relationship into another, and how it was necessary for us to examine our feelings closely instead of trusting their surface appearance. She was still feeling miserable and lonely. "I wish I was dead. No one would come to my funeral anyway, but I care only that Jesus would hold my hand."

She felt freer to cry in subsequent interviews, regardless of her "Indian" origin. Every now and then she would shyly address me as "Daddy," correcting herself with a pointed apology to "Dr. Ray." I tried to use this attachment to steer her toward more self-control. She was restless and began talking about running away again. I told her that I had assured the superintendent that she would not escape. "Well," she responded, "I had better stay here so that I don't put you to shame."

When I told her that I would be seeing her for six more weeks before my final departure from the institution she became uneasy and agitated, even cried a little. "How am I to get along here without you?" was her concern. Her behavior in the cottage and school became less appropriate, as reflected in the deterioration of her posttherapy ratings. My impression, confirmed by experiences with some of the other girls, was that she should have continued in therapy at least a year for about a hundred interviews to produce some stable effects.

104

Test Changes

MMPI: *K* (66-53), *Hy* (48-61), *Mf* 74-57, *A* (5-13), *At* (9-16), *Cn* (27-22) *Ca* (8-18), *Ho* (13-19), *Ad* (30-19)
16PF: *O* 8-4, *Q1* 3-8
HGI: *Ho* (23-38), *A* (1-5), *B* (O-6), *D* (O-5), *H* 7-4
HOW: *Tr* (76-95), *Cr* (67.5-92)

The majority of marked psychological changes in Olga indicate that the therapy was terminated before she obtained help in sealing the conflicts opened by interviews. Her defenses had been partially removed, making her more excitable, anxious and hostile. Despite aroused pathological trends there were some gains in her becoming more secure, less rigid in handling issues, and less oppressed by inappropriate guilt feelings.

Comments

In the preceding summaries of case histories, the behavior exhibited, the emotional states, and the reactions of the girls indicate clearly that they were seriously maladjusted. They exhibited immaturity beyond what is normal for an adolescent; their lack of inner controls, as well as the intensity and inappropriateness of their emotional responses showed disturbed pathological personality developments. Some of them were in need of extended psychotherapeutic treatment and belonged in a mental hospital rather than in a corrective institution. No diagnosis can be reliably made at this early stage of their pathology, but an attempt at classification may be given tentatively:

Neurotic:	Emma, Judy, Mary
Character disorder:	Ann, Betty, Cora, Dora, Fay, Grace, Kate, Lou, Nora
Latent schizophrenic:	Hanna, Olga

The diagnosis is particularly inconclusive between neurotics and character disorders. All of them had a neurotic core of emotional trauma and guilt feelings; all of them also acted out in disregard of social rules or authority. The diagnosis of neurosis was made if the neurotic insecurity and suffering were manifest and intense.

A similar view is expressed by Lampl-De Groot (1949): ". . . most of the cases show a combination of symptoms. The delinquent reveals neurotic trends, and our neurotic patients show tendencies toward more or less dissocial behavior. Therefore we are reduced to the quantitative aspects in making our diagnosis. Where the dissocial behavior predominates, we speak of a delinquent with neurotic symptoms; and where there is a reversed balance of factors, we speak of a neurotic personality with (often concealed) delinquent features."

One of the reasons for the confused boundaries between neurotics and character disorders was that the institutional controls did not allow the discharge of tensions in the ways possible in the family and in the community. Instead of finding outlets for aggression and sexuality, these institutionalized delinquents had to contain the promptings within themselves. In this way their symptomatology changed from alloplastic (Eissler, 1949), i.e., behaviorally expressed, to autoplastic, i.e., converted into neurotic symptoms of anxiety, depression, depersonalization, et cetera.

All the girls had been exposed to traumatic family environments: irresponsible and rejecting parents, particularly mothers; disrupted homes; sexual overstimulation; harmful examples; lack of limits; unmitigated sibling rivalry. The failures at school and conflicts with community authorities had further embittered them. They were cynical and apprehensive about human relationships. However, only in the case of Nora, and possibly Emma, did such disappointments disrupt the relationship with the therapist. The others were strongly attached to therapy, if not also to the therapist.

The psychotherapy was carried out in the manner I found most feasible in the institutional setting. Rigid experimental patterns, like meeting twice a week throughout the experimental period, or a minimum of twenty interviews, were abandoned early in the experiment. Such strict rules were considered more as guide lines than criteria for inclusion of subjects in the research. It was the clinical observations and conditions that determined the procedures rather than a preconceived rule.

Although I tried to maintain as intensive and regular contacts as possible, the interaction between me and the girls was always a

106

primary consideration. In a few cases I lost confidence that my more intensive effort would bear fruit in a better personality reaction, in which case the continuation and frequency of interviews was left entirely to the girls without suggestion or pressure of expectations which I used in more hopeful cases.

At the time of working with these subjects I was not aware that my "permissive" attitude in poorly responding cases might have been interpreted by them as rejection. In retrospect, I wonder whether my occasionally lukewarm attitude might have been interpreted as disinterestedness by the girls, impeding their progress and creating the feeling that I did not care about them just as other adults in the past had not cared.

The main method of achieving changes in the girls was considered to be helping them comply with the reasonable demands of training and discipline, and accept the stresses of their situation without overreacting. The changes in behavior shown in concrete institutional situations were considered as the beginnings of an attitudinal reorientation and partial personality change which might carry over into their community life. The main facilitating factor in changing them appeared to be a warm, respectful and, when necessary, frank but not a bluntly disapproving relationship between them and the therapist.

No open pressure was made for desirable changes, but they were not left in uncertainty as to which behavior I considered more mature and desirable. It was always clearly implied that I considered them capable of acceptable behavior according to their better judgment and conscience. This faith in them as dignified human beings was rarely verbalized; it was expressed as a basic attitude on my part.

Friendly laughter, a chat, small talk, were used as a technique to help the girls relax. Pauses were left undisturbed up to three minutes, depending on how uncomfortable they (and sometimes I) were with the silence. The motivational tendencies existing in the girls at the beginning and even later in therapy were utilized as foundations for any additional building or awakening of new personality trends. Most common trends were unhappiness about the present situation or hopelessness about the future; discomforts of guilt feelings and anxiety; ambitions toward self-affirmation and self-respect; fear of punishment for impulsive behavior; dependency needs and yearning for a satisfactory relationship with a helpful adult; relief from inner pressures through ventilation of anger or despair.

By some standards, this type of psychotherapy may not be considered "deep" enough. It certainly did not deal with deeply buried unconscious promptings and their derivatives. When I tried it, with Sandra, it did not do much good in modifying her behavior. Yet I dealt with matters pertinent to the girls, but often inaccessible to their awareness. The important question about psychotherapy need not be "depth" as defined by "dynamic" psychology, but effectiveness in modifying emotional and behavioral misdevelopments.

Glasser (1965—*Reality Therapy*) points out: "The question of 'depth' of the therapy is meaningless. It is interesting to hear both lay and trained people discuss therapy, saying that a certain psychiatrist does 'deep' therapy or that another one doesn't. As will be explained later, psychotherapy is only one thing. If it works at all to help the patient develop a more effective ego, it is 'deep' therapy. If it doesn't work, it can be as 'deep as the ocean' with no benefit to the patient. 'Superficial' or 'surface' therapy doesn't describe anything unless it conveys the meaning that the therapy is not effective."

The therapy described here represents at best only a limited beginning of the reconstruction of personality. Twenty or even fifty interviews served only as a foundation on which further improvements could be built by the girls and their adult guides. It became clear, through some parole failures of girls who had appeared improved clinically, that the gains in psychotherapy would be consolidated only if the therapist followed them in their community life.

The institutional conditions appeared to be both hampering and fostering changes through psychotherapy. On the detrimental side, it became clear that in many cases the institutional situation is too limited for free choice of behavior, for it is too artificial and too controlled to allow experiments with freedom. On the other hand I became convinced in the course of more than two years of experience with psychotherapy in the institution that the institutional frustrations and limits definitely pressured many girls to consider therapy more seriously as a refuge. I am rather certain that I could not have otherwise started psychotherapy or carried it beyond a few interviews with some of the present subjects. They remained in therapy only because institutional pressures raised the levels of their anxiety and hostility.

The pain of court commitment and the shock of having to behave within clearly prescribed limits, with promptly enforced punishments, created an atmosphere conducive to personality change. The learning in psychotherapy was speeded by the mental pain, worry, and discomfort caused by institutionalization. I was able to assume a nonauthoritative role with these delinquent youngsters because others were responsible for enforcing desired behavior; otherwise I would have had to abandon my benevolent role to prevent impulsive and self-destructive behavior. For this reason I decided that if I were to continue therapy with these girls on parole, I ought not to be engaged in a controlling or directing relationship. Desirable behavior should be enforced by the authority of the parole agents while the therapist reinforced rational and moral self-controls.

I considered my nonauthoritative role essential for the free flow of interactions between myself and the girls. It is true that I could not escape my position as an "officer" of the institution, but this role was minimized in the perception of the girls as they experienced my essentially nonjudgmental attitudes. Pressed by the consistent and unrelenting demands of the training personnel, the girls used interviews as a refuge where they could relax without fear and take fresh stock of themselves. Even strongly suspicious and apprehensive girls used their interviews for the relief of pent-up emotions, although they could not yet bring themselves to examine more closely their underlying intimate feelings.

Therapy may counteract some of the influences of institutional training by detaching the girls from the peer culture and from subservience to rebellious inmates and by helping them identify more meaningfully with socially desirable roles. Buehler and associates (1966) found that institutions unwittingly tend to reinforce antisocial patterns as inmates become trained to act within delinquent norms. Several of the present subjects have shown a separation from delinquent mores and an independence from pressures of peers in the institution.

One general conclusion is inescapable, after looking at the sordid life experiences of these tormented teenagers: They had been caught in the social, moral, and spiritual deterioration of our times; they were the victims of our crisis in values; their parents have grown into or accepted as their mental pattern hedonistic view that pleasures and personal wishes are the supreme guide in life. Moral teachings—requiring self-denial in the name of higher values—were unimportant in their motivations; yearnings for sexual pleasures, alcohol, and freedom from obligations seemed uppermost in their promptings. The natural consequence of such moral immaturity were incest, physical and emotional abuse of children, and a feeling of meaningless existence—all poor identification models for the growing girls.

The conventional psychotherapy currently dominated by the Freudian confusion as to the role of moral values in the healthy functioning of a personality can hardly be of much benefit to these discontented girls. My experience in working with them unequivocally indicated that their strongest need was for the inculcation of worthwhile goals to raise their self-respect and help them control their immature drives. In order to become "normal," these girls had to adopt "normal" (more or less conventional) thinking and behavior patterns. The institution stood rightly for these "conservative" views. I certainly was no adherent of nebulous ethical concepts of unqualified "self-expression" and freedom from social demands. In this respect, my therapeutic work was integrated with the institutional training.

PART II

RESEARCH REPORT ON
PSYCHOTHERAPY OF DELINQUENT GIRLS IN
AN INSTITUTION

RESEARCH REPORT ON PSYCHOTHERAPY
OF DELINQUENT GIRLS IN AN INSTITUTION

INTRODUCTION:

The Uncertainty About Effects of Psychotherapy

The effect of psychotherapy appears to be one of the poorly investigated areas of psychiatry and psychology. The literature on the subject is voluminous; the faith in the value of psychotherapy is confidently stated, but there is little in numerous reports and articles to convince the scientific skeptic. Stevenson (1959), a psychiatrist writing in the *American Journal of Psychiatry,* calls this lack of scientifically acceptable proofs the "major scandal of our profession:

"That psychotherapy of various kinds or of our favorite kind helps mental patients remains an important conviction of most of us. But with our present data such a conviction can hardly amount to more than an opinion among any who adhere to the principles of science. Many physicians of the 17th to 19th centuries had convictions about the efficacy of phlebotomy, but who bleeds patients today? The history of medicine, and of our own specialty particularly, shows that personal conviction provides an insufficient basis for therapeutic action, especially when danger or expense occur with the therapy. Harm rarely comes from psychotherapy, but expense nearly always. Considering the millions of dollars annually invested in it by patients and psychiatrists, by teachers and trainees, that we have almost no satisfactory studies of its results is a major scandal of our profession."

One of the sternest critics of the unsupported claims of psychotherapists, Eysenck (1952, 1961, 1964), finds little proof for

113

the usefulness of psychotherapy. Of the four experimental studies which Eysenck finds acceptable, i.e., those with properly established control groups, three show no significant results; of the fourth, which purports to show the effectiveness of client-centered therapy, Eysenck doubts that the control group was comparable to the therapy group.

The arguments of Eysenck may seem farfetched to a subjectively assured practitioner of psychotherapy, but they cannot be dismissed by a mere shrug of the shoulders and by taking recourse to belief. The only effective answer can come through well designed studies.

Eysenck (1961) acclaims *The Cambridge-Somerville Youth Study* (Powers and Witmer, 1951), as one of the best executed research projects on the effects of psychotherapy. Because the *Study* has a bearing on the research reported herein, it is worth reviewing in some detail. The *Study* used a large number of subjects, 325 in the course of ten years. The subjects were boys 6 to 12 years of age, with a median age of 10.5. The boys were selected for psychotherapy on the basis of their predelinquent status as determined by professional workers acquainted with their behavior and family circumstances. A matched group of boys was used as the control for the experimental youngsters who were treated by friendly relationship, advice, guidance, and help in concerns of health, education, and problems of adjustment. The experimental subjects were exposed to contacts with paid visitors who acted somewhat as Big Brothers. These counselors sought to "arouse socially sound values." The median duration of these "directed friendships" was five years. There were, on the average, 14 contacts with the boys alone, and 17 contacts with the boys and their families. Regular contacts were discontinued when the boys reached their seventeenth birthday.

Evaluation of the results of treatment was carried out three years after termination. The primary criterion for evaluation of the results of therapy was of a social nature: occurence of delinquency, seriousness of offenses, court appearances, and sentences. About two thirds of the counseled youngsters were kept out of trouble, apparently a considerable achievement. The counselors felt that they had done a good job. Most youngsters were appreciative of the help received. Yet the overall conclusion of the study is that individual counseling does not contribute significantly to a

114

reduction in delinquency. The reason for the discouraging conclusion is that the control group results show how misleading might be the claims based on the treatment group alone. Comparison between the control and treatment groups brings out the hard fact that the improvement and frequency of delinquency is at about the same level in both the counseled and the noncounseled boys. The only differences in favor of the counseled boys is that their offenses were less serious. The ratings of adjustment of the two groups show them to be at about the same level. Other evaluational devices show the counseled group to be somewhat better than the control group, but the small differences in group means rarely reach statistical significance.

These outcomes are hard to reconcile with the subjective impressions of both counselors and counselees that the relationship had been definitely beneficial. Dr. F. Allport poses a pertinent question in his Foreword to the *Study*: "Are the evaluative procedures just too crude to determine subtle gains in character and growth?" He feels that the antisocial conduct is a fallible criterion and that it may mask gains in emotional stability. Such a hope finds only tenuous support in the data of the *Cambridge-Sommerville Youth Study* report. The lack of significant differences in more detailed ratings and test scores has important implications for the research presented in this report.

Two evaluative surveys were carried out within the *Study*. One was conducted at an average of thirty one months subsequent to the beginning of treatment, the other five years after the inception of therapy. In the first survey, the experimental group showed no significant improvement on 14 rating scales, tests, and school and police records. In the second survey, 14 different evaluative criteria were used. The counseled group showed significant improvement on 4 of the 14 scales: Ethical Discrimination, Honesty, Vocabulary, and the Game of Threes ("Things you like to do? Things afraid of? Things you want to do for your family?"). The first survey contained a mixture of boys who were judged by the counselors to have profited the most and the least from treatment. Even when only the most benefited youngsters were considered, the scores were still not significantly more favorable for the experimental than for the non-counseled group. The second survey consisted only of boys who were most intensely treated; this may explain some significant improvements over the control group.

Although the results of the *Cambridge-Sommerville Youth Study* throw serious doubt on the basic usefulness of such an expensive and time-consuming effort as individual counseling in reducing delinquency, the research reported here had a sufficient number of distinguishing features to make it worth the venture. It was expected that the following differences between the *Study* and this research might produce different reactions to therapy:

   a) Sex of subjects: girls *vs.* boys.
   b) Circumstances: exposure to institutional pressures *vs.* disturbing parental and community influences.
   c) Psychotherapeutic method: office *vs.* home contacts; two interviews a week by a clinical psychologist *vs.* about monthly or bimonthly contacts over a period of years by social workers.
   d) Evaluative criteria: mostly psychological tests *vs.* delinquent records and rating scales.

The tentative results of another large study (Rudoff, 1959) do not appear to forecast a favorable outcome for the research presented here. The PICO (Pilot Intensive Counseling Organization) Project includes somewhat older male offenders, 18-22 years of age, in a California Correctional and Vocational Institution. The conduct ratings of the group counseled by the staff of social workers are, on the whole, not better than the offenders left to the routine vocational training. When the ratings are broken up into categories the experimental group is significantly higher in ratings only in the "outstanding" category. There are no differences in utilization of vocational training, and the data on recidivism of the two groups are inconclusive (experimental subjects staying a month longer on parole than members of the control group.)

Of particular interest for this study is the lack of significant changes on the scale of the California Psychological Inventory and the Minnesota Multiphasic Personality Inventory. The MMPI was used as one of the evaluation criteria in the present research. Rudoff and Bennett (1958) report no reliable changes in personality reactions from test to retest on either experimental or control groups in their large number of subjects.

Eysenck (1961) also quotes a number of studies on comparative statistics which seem to indicate no significant difference in

116

the improvement of treated and untreated psychotics and neurotics. The criteria were the global ratings of the psychotherapists involved with the patients, or the absence of repeated hospitalization in a period of two years. Again, the question of appropriateness or criteria may be raised; the ratings are notoriously unreliable even when performed by uninvolved and well trained raters. (Forer *et al.*, 1961) The avoidance of hospitalization may be only a very rough criterion of emotional stability, psychological comfort, or smoother problem solving which might have resulted from psychotherapy. Eysenck remarks: "It is possible, or course, that effects were looked for in the wrong quarter; psychotherapy may affect personality traits and behavior patterns other than those relevant to psychiatric improvement as ordinarily understood." What seems necessary is to evaluate psychotherapy effects along refined dimensions rather than global ones. Such an approach was used in the present study through the employment of numerous test scales.

The effects of individual psychotherapy on behavioral and psychological changes in institutionalized juvenile delinquents, i.e., those between 12 and 18 years of age, have been even less systematically investigated. The review of literature in the years 1949-1967 reveals only one study (Watt, 1949) of individual therapy with a control group in the research design. The remainder of the reports are based on clinical impressions and ratings of the participating psychiatrists or psychologists, or upon known recidivism or court appearances. Such evaluative procedures can hardly settle questions posed by those skeptical of the effects of psychotherapy in general, and psychotherapy with institutionalized offenders in particular.

Watt (1949) used a design basically similar to the one employed in the present study. He selected a group of 22 delinquent boys at the Utah State School, divided them at random into experimental and control groups, and applied the nondirective counseling with 11 experimental subjects. He found that 6 of them improved on all the interview ratings of insight, free decision, free expression, and action. He also found that the counseled subjects improved significantly over the control subjects on 3 MMPI scores and on 3 scores of the California Test of Personality.

Some well executed studies report the effects of group therapy

117

or a combination of group and individual therapy.

Shelly and Johnson (1961) used a group of 50 somewhat older young offenders as subjects of their experiment. They were exposed to intensive counseling work, consisting of about thirty-eight hours of individual counseling and fifty-two of group counseling and numerous brief contacts according to the needs of offenders living in a workcamp. The control group consisted of offenders in another workcamp where the training was not combined with counseling. Both the experimental and the control group were administered 7 cards of the Thematic Apperception Test a few weeks after they entered the training and about six months later. The responses were scored for the presence of antisocial themes. The counseled group showed a reduction in antisocial themes significant at the .02 level of probability when compared with the noncounseled group. That the reduction in antisocial themes corresponds with an improvement in social controls is evident from the follow-up study: the offenders from both groups who showed a larger reduction in antisocial scores on TAT cards had a record of better parole adjustment.

Truax (1966) investigated the effects of psychotherapy on 40 delinquent institutionalized girls interviewed in groups twice a week for three months. The girls in treatment showed significant improvement on 13 scales on the Minnesota Counseling Inventory, an improvement not evident with the control group. Of particular importance was the improvement on the delinquency scale of the Inventory. The adjustment of girls who participated in treatment was also better outside the institution, judged by their longer stay on parole. Truax suggests that the chief reason for the effectiveness of treatment in this case—in contrast to the poor results obtained in other attempts—lies in the quality of therapy offered. He contends that "average therapy" may fail with delinquents, and that good psychotherapy" succeeds. He defines "good" therapy as high in accurate empathy and positive regard.

Persons (1966) investigated the effects of what might be considered intensive psychotherapy in an institutional setting. Group interviews were conducted with 41 delinquent boys, average age 16 years, twice a week. In addition each boy was seen once a week, and sometimes more often in individual psychotherapy. The program was carried on for twenty weeks and psychological tests readministered to both the therapy and matched control groups. The treatment group showed improvement far superior to that of the youngsters exposed only to institutional training. The experimental group improved significantly at $p=.001$ on all clinical MMPI scales (except *Ma,* $p=.002$), on the Taylor Anxiety Scale, and on two delinquency measures. The control group was significantly *higher* on both a delinquency scale and the scale of emotionally inappropriate responsivity (*Sc*). These psychological test results were accompanied by behavioral improvement of the therapy subjects: they had fewer disciplinary infractions, did better in school, and received their passes sooner.

These three studies indicate that group psychotherapy with offenders is likely to lead to greater increases in socialized and mature behavior than institutional training alone. It is presumed here that individual therapy would be more effective than group psychotherapy. However, this opinion is not shared by all psychotherapists. There is no agreement among those who tried to help offenders psychotherapeutically as to the best method applicable or the effects to be expected. Slavson (1947), Shulman (1952), and Hill (1953) consider group therapy counterindicated for offenders and character disorders. Beukenkamp (1958) and Sohn (1952) make an opposing recommendation, disclaiming the effectiveness of individual therapy with character disturbances.

Some experts doubt the usefulness of any therapy with character disorders and antisocial individuals particularly if they are in institutions. For example, an experienced worker with offenders, Melitta Schmideberg (1955), finds that neither group nor individual psychotherapy is of much avail with institutionalized individuals. She feels that the psychotherapeutic effect with them is made ineffective by the punitive aspects of institutions. Inmates, she finds, are likely to associate the therapist with the irritating institutional practices, so that psychotherapy would be countered by attendant punitive experiences. She recommends treatment when the offenders are in the community, on parole, or on probation.

TABLES

1. Homogeneity of Therapy (T) and Nontherapy (C) Groups on the Three Essential Matching Variables. 123

2. The Initial Characteristics of Therapy (T) and the Nontherapy (C) Groups. 136

3. Mean Ratings on the HOW Behavior Rating Schedule for T and C Groups at Pretherapy (Pr) and Posttherapy (Po) Evaluation. 137

4. Means of T and C Groups on Clinical and Additional MMPI Scales at the Pretherapy (Pr) and Posttherapy (Po) Testing. 140

5. Means of T and C Groups on the Sixteen Personality Factor Questionnaire at the Pretherapy (Pr) and Posttherapy (Po) Testing. 141

6. Means of T and C Groups on the Self and Ideal Self Sortings, and Their Discrepancies at the Pretherapy (Pr) and Posttherapy (Po) Testing. 142

7. Means of T and C Groups on the Hostility Guilt Index Scales at the Pretherapy (Pr) and Posttherapy (Po) Testing. 143

8. Means of T and C Groups on the KD Proneness Scales at the Pretherapy (Pr) and Posttherapy (Po) Testing 144

9. Means of T and C Groups on the Rorschach Indices at the Pretherapy (Pr) and Posttherapy (Po) Testing. 145

10. Sums of Ratings of the T and C Groups on the Rating Schedule of Parole Adjustment. 154

RESEARCH REPORT

Problem

The main hypothesis to be verified by this study was that there is a significantly larger psychological and behavior improvement in institutionalized delinquent girls who are treated in individual psychotherapy than those exposed only to the institutional training.

Methods and Procedures

Basic Design

The experimental design basically consists in comparing psychological and behavior changes in two groups of 14 experimental and 14 control subjects. The criteria of evaluation were a behavior rating scale, 6 psychological tests, and a Parole Adjustment Rating Schedule.

Selection of Subjects

The experimental subjects were selected for psychotherapy from girls referred to me by institutional personnel—the superintendent, social worker, nurse, cottage counselors. The reasons for referral usually were slow adaptation to training demands and disciplinary measures; open aggressiveness; incongruent or strikingly immature behavior; prolonged periods of depression, and suicidal gestures. These girls represented the more maladjusted individuals. They had been more severely traumatized in their childhood, and were usually more violent or inappropriate in their acting-out than the average delinquent in the institution.

Only girls committed for the first time to the correctional institution were subjects of research. They were advised that counseling might help them handle their troubles with less emotional upset and they were prompted to decide about entering counseling after thinking about it for a few days. Most of them made the decision in the first interview. None of the girls expressing the desire to come for regular counseling was rejected. A few of the subjects had to wait for two or three weeks to start regularly scheduled interviews.

The control or nontherapy subjects were chosen from a selected portion of the school population, i.e., those girls who expressed willingness to avail themselves of counseling. The inquiry sheet regarding their interest in obtaining psychological help can be found in Appendix I. It seemed important to match the experimental and control subjects on this variable, for some published research indicates that those who reject psychological counseling might be persons with different personality makeup than those who are willing to enter a psychotherapeutic relationship (Rogers and Dymond, 1954). The control subjects were matched with therapy subjects on the basis of the following three essential criteria:

    a) Age—within two years.
    b) Time spent in the institution prior to first testing—within two months.
    c) IQ—within 10 points on the Henmon-Nelson Test of Mental Maturity.

Two additional matching criteria (described in Appendix VI) also were attempted and largely achieved:

    d) Family background—achieved in 13 pairs.
    e) Level of delinquency—achieved in 12 pairs.

The matching of the girls by cottages in which they lived was not attempted for it was found to be impractical. It would have severely limited the matching possibilities on account of the small selection of subjects available and created complications when some of the subjects were occasionally moved from one cottage to another. Both the experimental and control subjects came from all the cottages of the institution.

The matching effectiveness is confirmed by data in Table 1. The test used for verifying the homogeneity of the groups is Wilcoxon Matched-Pairs Signed-Ranks Test (Siegel, 1956), which was utilized for determining the significance of differences throughout this report. Only the IQ differences appear systematicaly higher within pairs for the experimental (therapy, T) group. However, the mean difference is numerically small, 2.3 IQ points. The median IQ was 97 for T group and 93 for the control (C) group.

Table 1

Homogeneity of Therapy (T) and Nontherapy (C) Groups on the Three Essential Matching Variables

Variable	Group		Mean
	T	C	Difference
Mean age, in months	192	188	4
Mean time in institution, months	4.4	4.4	0
IQ	97.4	95.1	2.3*

*p=.05

Psychotherapeutic Method

The descriptions of the psychotherapeutic method employed in this study are given in some detail in order to provide the reader with as operational a definition of the processes employed as possible. This was deemed necessary because at present there are many methods and approaches subsumed under the vague term of psychotherapy. The treatment summaries given in Part I defined by examples the method utilized in this research.

The guidelines for the psychotherapy employed here were taken from a summary Welsch (1957) made of a series of lectures on the treatment of adolescents:

Basic agreement seemed to be in the following areas: (1) that extraordinary flexibility of approach is required on the part of the therapist treating an adolescent; (2) that orthodoxy of technique, of whatever specific type, is rarely usable in toto in the treatment of adolescent; (3) that analysis of the psychodynamics of the adolescent's biographical past is rarely appropriate or successful in treatment of adolescents, although unresolved problems of childhood are to be seen

123

by the therapist as contributing to the turbulence of adolescence and weakening his adaptive capacities during that period; (4) that supporting and strengthening of ego function is most appropriate in therapy with adolescents; (5) that the adolescent most frequently utilizes the therapeutic approach related to his current and immediate concerns; (6) the adolescents are exceptionally labile emotionally, and therapy is directed toward helping the adolescent develop objectivity and more stable and mature value judgments about his own behavior in relation to present reality situations; (7) that the changes accompanying sexual maturation offer new realities with which the adolescent has to cope; (8) that treatment of adolescents differs in technical approach from that of children or of adults but utilizes some of the techniques of each; (9) that treatment of the adolescent is usually shorter in duration (than that of psychoanalysis of adults); (10) that parents exist and require attention to varying degrees in the interest of successful pursuit of therapy for the adolescent; (11) that the adolescent's need for and view of the therapist as a helping person has unique qualities, and the therapist needs to be sensitive to the role and meaning he or she has for the adolescent in order to avoid certain pitfalls and at the same time to represent a stable, empathic maturity which offers opportunity for the adolescent's own reality testing; (12) that regardless of the specific technique used and the immediate urgency dealt with by the adolescent, a full dynamic understanding of the adolescent's physical status, personality structure, and adaptive patterns is required on the part of the therapist.

A basic guide for treatment was my general understanding of delinquent personality. I saw these youngsters primarily as character disorders who have not learned socialized, mature, and effective ways of coping with frustrations. Their reactions to impulsive promptings and desires usually took the form of uninhibited expression and self-indulgence. If they were to live in society without serious conflicts, they needed to accept self-limitation as the best policy in the long run. They had to accept short-term frustrations if they were to avoid long-term troubles for themselves and members of their present and future families.

In contrast to neurotics, who usually internalize their frustrations, these young disordered characters were externalizing them. Neurotics tend to act at the expense of their satisfactions; delinquents at the expense of others, of social norms, or of their own conscience. Neurotics may need a freer expression of some impulses; delinquents need more repression, or temporary renouncement at any rate. Neurotics may need to renounce their compulsive trends, and delinquents to correct their irresponsibility and disregard of social mores.

The overall therapeutic goals toward which I strived in the course of the interviews were emotional reeducation, personality integration, and acceptance of socially approved behavior. I tried to:

a) Establish a relationship that would demonstrate the respect of an adult for these young people as persons.

b) Provide an opportunity for ventillation of tension and catharsis.

c) Minimize their impulsive acting-out. Their hasty acts were shown as useless and harmful to them as part of an immature system of dealing with environment. They were induced to resist surrendering to strong feelings; to postpone action until they could see what results it might bring them; and to think first and act later; they were helped to accept controls, limitations, and frustrations as part of the general pattern of living—one which has to be accepted, or which might be changed by some successful problem-solving approach.

d) Reduce hampering feelings of guilt and anxiety. They were taught to accept the "unworthy" impulses of sex and hostility as part of a natural human conflict between some values and some pleasures without being dominated or agitated by unacceptable desires; to become detached from neurotic concentration on past failures, and to seize chances offered by the present and the future; to experience warmth, trust, and respect for their personality so that the inordinate anxiety about themselves and their environment could be largely dissipated; to relax some of the unjustified self-blame for conflicts with parents, adults, authorities; to establish the primacy of superego and of personal values as the compass in life. Bilmes (1965), and others have argued that delinquency is primarily an attempt to escape the conscience. Teaching delinquents to come to terms with conscience could be expected, then, to have therapeutic results.

125

e) Lead to insights about their antisocial or harmful drives. They were helped to consider their past experiences in the home and community. Some of their bitterness and overreacting were minimized for the girls were desensitized to some of the past stimuli. However, I made no attempt to bring the girls to a clear awareness of their underlying unconscious motivations. Truax and Carkhuff (1965) later validated the correctness of such psychotherapeutic moderation. They found that the degree of self-exploration was correlated positively with change in general neuropsychiatric patients, but negatively in delinquents.

f) Help build up realistic goals for education, work, family living, sex, marriage, community service, dealing with temptations, et cetera.

In short, I led them to lean on me, to borrow strength from my more mature ego and superego till they became disentangled from some of their conflicting feelings. For a time I was their "substitute ego."

The technique used in the interviews was a conversational approach and trying to pick up leads from any statement a subject might make or asking what was on her mind if she were unusually silent. The subjects were encouraged to bring up any of their feelings freely. A friendly, warm, accepting attitude was maintained at all times, but I did not hide my disagreement with over-emotional and immature reactions. If they felt restless and agitated they were free to pace the room or stare through the window. In order to facilitate the immediacy of my reaction and to minimize the possible suspiciousness of the subjects, no notes were taken during the interviews. Condensed notes were written after the interviews.

In the initial interview the subjects were informed about what they might expect from counseling, warned against premature disappointments, but told that they could stop coming to talk with me any time they felt like it. They were told it would be desirable to come for about three months, and that they could decide at that time whether they wanted to continue. They were assured that the interviews were confidential, and that their statements would not be communicated to any institutional authorities —unless they planned to run away or harm themselves or someone else. These exceptions to confidentiality were represented as protection against their failing in good judgment.

I never inquired about things girls were reluctant to talk about. I did ask questions concerning their delinquencies as well as other matters of their past lives, but I never pursued these topics if the subjects showed that they would rather not continue the discussion. I only commented: "Apparently you do not care to go further into this problem at present."

This abstention from probing was decided upon deliberately. The main reason was that pointed questioning was apt to remind girls of police investigators. As if to warn me against intruding questions, several subjects told me that they had not liked psychiatrists who had asked them personal questions in the course of diagnostic interviews. Another important reason for avoiding probing was the likelihood of hastening sexual transference or veiled erotic fantasy during interviews. Despite this precaution, some of the subjects told me stories which were veiled seductive encouragements.

The pressure to reveal thought contents was also avoided because a complete review of past or even present experiences was not considered essential to therapy. The spontaneity of communication was considered more useful for the emotional comfort and stabilization of the subjects than making them aware of all the antecedents to their present reactions and habits. Rogers and associates (1948) have demonstrated that human behavior is influenced more by their understanding of environment, their phenomenological orientation, than by the environmental impact and by their experiences in the past. Rogers (1964, p. 125) comments on those findings.

"When we examined only the delinquents who came from the most unfavorable homes and remained in those homes, it was still true that their future behavior was best predicted, not by the unfavorable conditioning they were receiving in their home environment, but by the degree of realistic understanding of themselves and their environment which they possessed. Thus the phenomenological vairable proved to be much more closely related to future behavior than the assessment of the observable external environment, and the stimuli it provided."

I was basically confident that real problems were bound to come up in interviews despite the resistive guardedness of the subjects. This conviction was found to be justified for most subjects. Whenever, against my better judgment, I tried to break down resistance by asking definite questions the result was only an increased apprehensiveness in a girl. Sometimes I had the impression that a number of interviews were wasted in defensive chatting or talking about superficial matters; and yet these interviews laid the ground for later uninhibited baring of deeper conflicts. When a girl was manifestly fearful or resistant, I usually limited myself to pointing out her stalling, interpreting it as an expected resistance, and reminding her that it was her hour and she could use it any way she wished but that hiding real feelings and thoughts was of no help to her.

It was surprising, and gratifying, that most of these traumatized and outwardly rebellious subjects quickly developed a trusting and warm relationship with me. Only two or three remainded guarded and somewhat distant, unable to overcome earlier disappointments with adults of their past, but even these subjects continued to come for the interviews as a means of solace and retreat from the pressures of institutional demands or personal grief and uncertainty. They often commented that by telling me about their tensions they were able to be better self-controlled and avoided punishment for impulsive acting-out. The usual relationship of a subject to me could best be characterized as that of daughter to a nonpunitive father. The sensual and sexual overtones of transference were occasionally in evidence.

I avoided a stereotyped role in the interviews, without trying to be too watchful, clever, analytical or superior. I was just myself, with the advantages and disadvantages of a nontechnical role. Most of the time I was an attentive, respectful listener; occasionally I responded emotionally. It was foreign to me to play the role considered by Eissler (1946b) to be essential in the therapy of delinquents: awe them by penetrating foresights; impress them as being one up on them in the game of delinquency. In such a role, I would have felt that manipulation and insincerity was detrimental to a trusting, friendly, and relaxed relationship. Neither did I think that it would be therapeutically useful to ally myself temporarily with the delinquent behavior of the psychopath, as Schwartz (1967) advocates.

The interviews were usually held twice a week, each for about fifty minutes. After 20 interviews the subjects were given the choice of coming twice weekly, once a week, or only occasionally. About half chose to continue with two interviews a week;

the others decided to handle situations more independently. Some of them explained that they thought they should get used to being without a therapist because he would not be available to them in the community; others expressed concern for "other girls who need help," whom I might start seeing in the time released by them.

The mean number of interviews held was 23.3; the median 25; the range 15-41. The mean time of psychotherapeutic contacts (between the pretherapy and posttherapy testing) was 5.2 months, median 6 months, range 2.5 to 9 months.

Two other variables are inextricably tied to the effects of therapy: The type of institutional training, and the therapist himself. These were described in the Introduction, but additional information on the therapist is relevant at this point.

The Therapist

There was only one therapist employed in the experiment, myself. The therapist's attitude, personality characteristics, training, and professional experience have been indicated as possibly being influential factors of psychotherapeutic outcomes. I felt a rather strong and positive identification with the girls. Although already in my forties, my feelings were resonant with the emotional turmoil of the adolescent phase of development of my subjects. Their social handicaps and family traumas brought up lively protective trends within me. I saw them as suffering from social injustice and parental deviation from mental health and maturity. I sensed an urgency about the psychotherapeutic work I was doing since these girls would be mothers in a few years, and would create havoc in the lives of their children similar to their own unless they found healthier ways of handing their feelings. Part of my attitude was derived from fifteen years of experience as a social group worker.

As to the psychotherapeutic training and experience I might have been rated as sufficiently well prepared for my task. I had conducted about 1,500 psychotherapeutic interviews by the time I started the experiment, about 1,000 of these being with the girls in the institution. I obtained only occasional supervision for my psychotherapeutic activities. My professional interest, and my doctoral dissertation (1958), are in the area of psychotherapy.

129

I had no personal analysis, and did not believe I needed it for this work. I do not share the exclusive theoretical outlook of any psychological school, and I am quite skeptical of the value of Freudian theory and practice. My approach to psychotherapy might be described as eclectic.

The Instruments of Evaluation

The criteria of evaluation were deliberately chosen so as to minimize contamination by my views and impressions, and for that reason a behavior rating schedule and six psychological tests were used in the experiment. The ratings and testings were accomplished at the pretherapy and posttherapy points for the experimental and matched subjects. No follow-up evaluation with all the tests and ratings was feasible. However, I assumed that the stability of psychological improvement in delinquents would be confirmed by investigation as it had been with adults (Rogers and Dymond, 1954) after individual therapy, and with male (Persons, 1967) and female (Truax, 1966) delinquents after group therapy.

(1) *Haggerty-Olson-Wickman* (1930) *Behavior Rating Schedules* (HOW)

The HOW was developed mainly to evaluate the aggressive, noncompliant trends in "problem children." The focus is on the physical, intellectual, social, and emotional traits of the subjects. Only the *B* portion of HOW was utilized in this research.

Each subject was rated by the classroom teacher and by two cottage counselors. The contact between teachers and counselors was minimal within the institution. The cottage counselors were asked to do their ratings independently; their ratings were pooled into one. No attempt was made at systematic training of raters in order to improve the reliability of ratings. The experimenter visited the counselors and teachers in the beginning to request them to do the ratings and answer any questions about the use of HOW which had been previously distributed to them.

(2) *Minnesota Multiphasic Personality Inventory* (MMPI)

The MMPI has been used extensively in research with juvenile delinquents. In that period I had carried out a standardization study of Clinical and additional scales of MMPI for the institutional population (Jurjevich, 1963), and another on MMPI scale changes concomitant with institutional training (1966a).

The clinical and 16 seemingly more appropriate additional scales were used to assess the changes in traits and psychopathological trends of the subjects.

(3) *Rorschach*

The Rorschach Ink Blot Test had been used in evaluation of psychotherapeutic outcome with equivocal results. Knopf (1956) reviewed several studies in which the whole test, or some of its categories, was employed in predicting or evaluating results of psychotherapy. The findings are meager and contradictory. Knopf's resigned explanation is: "Maybe we are expecting more sensitivity and clarity than our present knowledge of both Rorschach and the process of psychotherapy would permit." The Rorschach was included in the test battery here as a trial tool, and only the numerical indices were used. The hypotheses developed for these indices were:

A. That the scores of the T group would be higher (more improved) than for the C group for the following categories:

1. Number of responses, R
2. Good form responses. $F+\%$
3. Human movement, M
4. Form-color responses, FC
5. Adequate, appropriate percepts, $+F\%$
6. Human content responses, $H\%$
7. "New Form" responses, $New\ F\%$
8. "New Form" responses, accurate or appropriate, $New\ F+\%$
9. Human to animal movement ratio, $M{:}FM$
10. Form-color to color-form ratio, $FC{:}\ CF+C$
11. Human to animal content ratio, $(H+Hd){:}\ (A+Ad)$
12. Higher popular concepts, P and $P\%$
13. Whole responses to human movement ratio, $W{:}M$

B. That the scores of the T group would be lower (i.e., less pathological) than for the C group for the following categories:

131

14. Number of rejections, *Rej*
15. Shading scores, combined (scores containing *c, K, k*)
16. Inadequate, inappropriate percepts, $-F\%$
17. Response time to gray cards (RTg), to colored cards (RTc) and the difference between them $(RTg\text{-}RTc)$
18. Percepts with animal content, $A\%$
19. Average time for responses, T/R
20. Rorschach Content Test (RCT) anxiety and RCT hostility.

The rationale and scoring techniques for the less frequently used categories are given in Appendix II. The scoring system applied was that of Klopfer (1954).

In addition to standard Rorschach, the Rorschach Content Test (RCT) was used for scores of anxiety and hostility. The RCT was developed by Elizur (1949). The scoring system employed here is that given by Elizur. The scoring of those content categories not explicitly listed by Elizur is given in Appendix III. The categories which appeared during the free-association and inquiry periods, as well as in spontaneous additional responses, were scored on RCT.

(4) *Sixteen Personality Factor Questionnaire* (16PF)
The 16PF was developed by Cattell and associates (1957). The names and description of the factors are supplied in Appendix V. The *Short Form C* was used in this research.

(5) *Kvaraceus Delinquency Proneness Scale* (KD)
The KD was developed by Professor W.C. Kvaraceus (1953), through his research in delinquency. The plus scores represent those found typically in delinquents. The minus scores are derived from items answered in that direction by nondelinquent youth. The total score is the difference between the plus and minus scores. The more a score is in the minus direction, the less likely is the subject to be delinquent.

(6) *Self and Ideal Q Sorts*
I developed a series of one hundred fifty statements, which were randomly assigned to three decks of fifty statements each.

The Q sort items were selected from a pool of 188 items. Except for 13 items taken from the Hartley-Butler sorts (Rogers and Dymond, 1954), the original items were compiled from my notes of interviews I had with girls in the institution. These 188 items were submitted to four clinical psychologists, with several years of post-Ph.D. experience with delinquents. They were asked to separate the items into those that indicated good and poor adjustment, and those of neutral adaptive meaning. The raters* agreed unanimously on 68 items as representing healthy self-concepts, and 68 standing for maladaptive self-concepts. The remaining 14 items were considered healthy or unhealthy by at least three raters; the fourth considered them neutral. The framework within which the ratings were carried out appears in "Notes to Raters," in Appendix IV. The same Appendix contains the sorting items.

The sorting was done by the subjects first on self concepts on all three decks, then on Ideal Self concepts. The instructions given to the subject appear in Appendix IV. The sorting scheme was designed to approximate a normal distribution:

	Most like me					*Least like me*			
Column number	9	8	7	6	5	4	3	2	1
Number of cards	2	3	6	9	10	9	6	3	2

The score on Self and Ideal Self was determined by the number of good adjustment items (item numbers 1-25, 51-75, 101-125) in columns 6-9, and maladjustment items (26-50, 76-100, 126-150) in columns 1-4. The cards placed in column 5 were not counted, being considered of no particular importance to the sorter. In this way the maximum score obtainable by a subject on each sort was 40.

(7) *Hostility Guilt Index* (HGI)**

The HGI was devised by Buss and Durkee (1953). The test is of a questionnaire type and contains the total hostility score, the *Ho*, and the following subscales: *A*—Assault; *B*—Indirect hostility; *C*—Irritability; *D*—Negativism; *E*—Resentment; *F*—Suspicion; *G*—hostility; *H*—Guilt.

---

* I am indebted to Drs. Bonnie Webb Camp, E. Ellis Graham, B. Lynn Harriman, and Chester Poremba for their cooperation in rating the items.
**I am grateful to Mr. George Levy for supplying me with the printed forms of the test.

Results

The dimension along which the effects of psychotherapy are measured in this research is the reduction of pathological trends and enhancement of adaptive characteristics within T and C groups.

An important question pertinent to the meaning of test results is whether the matching procedure had succeeded in creating groups comparable along psychological dimensions. In fact a point that to me seems crucial, is the verification of the assumption that, on the whole, the group in therapy did not initially represent healthier individuals than the control group. A healthier individual can be expected to utilize more effectively the opportunities for personal growth through institutional training than a conflicted, maladjusted personality. Maladjusted personalities are usually more rigid, sensitive, apprehensive, aggressive, impulsive, and irrational, and they are more apt to take negativistic stands toward efforts at their reeducation.

Table 2 compares the initial behavioral and psychological status of the T and C groups along several dimensions. On the whole, the T group is more severely maladjusted to begin with; however, the pathological indices are significantly higher in the T than in C group only on the following two scales: latent hostility (RCT) and delinquency (Dq). T group is better than C group in only one dimension: a more realistic ideal sell as reflected on sortings of Deck I. The behaviorial ratings were significantly worse for the T group, but that is as it should be expected for the girls were referred to the therapist because of their manifestly poorer adaptation and the failure of institutional methods to influence them. The three statistically significant initial psychological differences do not throw serious doubt on the comparability of the T and C groups. In the 24 scales checked, the appearance of three significant differences at the .05 level of probability could have occured in about twelve cases in a hundred (Wilkinson, 1951). It appears that the three psychological differences could have arisen by chance and may not represent an actual difference between T and C group.

134

It is important to note that the defensive answers on objective tests are about equal in both groups, as seen in the nonsignificant scores on scales of denial (*Dn*) and of social desirability (*So-r*).

It can be concluded from Table 2 that the matching procedures produced psychologically equivalent groups, indistinguishable along a large number of psychological dimensions.

There is another possible explanation for reduction in pathological scores which could throw doubt on the hypothesis that the therapeutic effects can account for lessened psychopathological trends. Such an explanation could be formulated as the possibility that the higher scores would lead automatically to lowered scores on retesting through regression toward the mean. Such a regression is observable on many tests. To check on this possibility, Spearman correlation coefficients—*rho*'s—were calculated on 3 scales showing significant differences between *T* and *C* groups on pretherapy and posttherapy tests (delinquency on MMPI, hostility on RCT, and behavioral ratings on HOW). The respective correlation coefficients for ranks of combined *T* and *C* initial and final scores were: .66, .58, and .38. These *rho*'s are significant at .001, .001 and .05 respectively, i.e., high scores do not tend to produce lower scores upon retesting.

A check was also carried out on two nonsignificantly different scales on initial tests of *T* and *C* groups, namely anxiety (*A*) of MMPI and hostility of HGI. Both coefficients are .41, significant at .01. These findings make unlikely the assumption that lower posttherapy scores of the more maladjusted *T* groups could be accounted for by their being initially higher. Another investigation of regression effects (Jurjevich, 1966c) also confirmed that they are not regularly proportional to the elevation of scores on self-reporting questionnaires.

TABLE 2

The Initial Characteristics of Therapy (*T*) and the Nontherapy (*C*) Groups

Negative Variable	Group Mean T	Group Mean C	Probability of Differences
1. HOW, rating by cottage counselors	85.7	80.8	.06
2. HOW, rating by teachers	84.0	72.7	NS
3. HOW, teachers and counselors combined	84.8	76.7	.02
4. RCT—hostility	4.2	1.7	.05
5. HGI—hostility	39.2	34.4	NS
6. MMPI, judged hostility, *Jh*	19.1	20.9	NS
7. RCT—anxiety	10.6	7.7	.07
8. MMPI, *A* factor scale, anxiety	20.7	18.1	NS
9. MMPI, psychopathic deviate, *Pd*	78.5	73.1	NS
10. MMPI, schizophrenic, *Sc*	66.8	66.4	NS
11. MMPI, denial of symptoms, *Dn*	11.4	11.2	NS
12. MMPI, social desirability, *So-r*	23.8	25.4	NS
13. MMPI, delinquency, *Dq*	16.0	13.0	.05
14. MMPI, dependency, *De*	27.2	30.0	NS
15. 16PF, suspiciousness, *L*	6.0	6.0	NS
16. Self-ideal sort, Deck I—unrealistic "ideal"	32.6	36.3	.02
17. Self-ideal sort, Deck II—unrealistic "ideal"	32.6	35.1	NS
18. Self-ideal sort, Deck III—unrealistic "ideal"	30.0	31.9	NS
19. Self sort, Deck I—self appraisal	25.0	30.1	NS
20. Self sort, Deck II—self appraisal	30.3	32.9	NS
21. Self sort, Deck III—self appraisal	28.0	29.2	NS
Positive Variable			
22. MMPI, ego strength scale, *Es*	38.3	40.4	NS
23. MMPI, admission of symptoms, *Ad*	21.1	24.1	NS
24. Rorschach, number of responses, *R*	23.9	21.2	NS
25. Rorschach, human movement, *M*	3.4	3.6	NS
26. Rorschach, new *F+%*	78.4	86.0	NS
27. Rorschach, popular, *P*	6.7	6.8	NS

Results of Behavioral Ratings

Table 3 shows that the behavioral improvement is judged to be much larger with T than with C group by both teachers and cottage counselors, although it does not quite reach the level of $p = .05$, which was adopted as the criterion of significance in this study. (The larger difference in the ratings of teachers appears statistically nonsignificant, and the smaller one for combined counselors and teachers as significant because of a peculiarity of the Wilcox test which takes into account the direction and size of differences between pairs and not the group means.) A larger difference in mean scores signifies a larger reduction in maladjusted scores from pre- to posttherapy testing.

TABLE 3

Mean Ratings on the HOW Behavior Rating Schedule for T and C Groups at Pretherapy (Pr) and Posttherapy (Po) Evaluation

Raters	T		C	
	Pr	Po	Pr	Po
Teachers	84.0	75.6[?]	72.7	71.0
Counselors	85.7	78.1	80.8	79.9
Teachers and Counselors	84.9	76.9*	76.7	75.5

Difference significant at *p = .05, ?p = .08

The trend toward rating individuals in therapy as having come nearer to the desirable adjustment can be also seen in the fact that teachers see 11 subjects in T group as improved and 3 as worse at the posttherapy rating; the counselors rate 9 improved, 5 as worse. The proportions for the C group are 7 improved and 7 worse in the ratings of both teachers and counselors.

The rating of 3 therapy subjects as worse by teachers, and 5 subjects as worse by counselors may be taken as an indication that the ratings on HOW were not decisively influenced by the knowledge that the girls were in therapy. The raters did not appear desirous to rate the therapy subjects more leniently in order not to disappoint the therapist. Some of the largest scores in deterioration between pretherapy and posttherapy points occurred on 3 subjects of T group—Fay, Mary, and Olga. If anything, the subjects of T group seemed to be rated more strictly, maybe because a better behavior was expected of them. In fact some of them reported that teachers and counselors had reprimanded them for not doing better in spite of taking up the psychologist's time.

It is of interest to note, in passing, that the cottage counselors are decidedly more strict as raters than are teachers. The mean pretherapy ratings of T group as 85.7 and 84, and of C group as 80.8 and 72.7 for counselors and teachers, respectively, are significantly $(p = .01)$ stricter for counselors. Whether this is because of the closer association of cottage counselors with the girls, or greater focussing of cottage personnel on comforming behavior cannot be ascertained from the data at hand.

MMPI Results

Table 4 provides information on mean differences between the changes of MMPI scales in T and C groups from pretherapy to posttherapy testing. The T group appears significantly improved in the following scales on which there is no significant change in C group: psychopathic deviate (Pd); delinquency (Dq); schizophrenia (Sc); manifest anxiety (At); A factor anxiety; excitability (Ca); repression (R); and social conformity in expressed opinions $(So\text{-}r)$. The C group is significantly improved on the ego strength (Es) scale, without a corresponding rise for T group. Also, the C group shows some tendency to deny symptoms (Dn) which are not exhibited by the T group. The T group shows a more significant improvement over the statistically confirmed improvement of the C group on the scales of oddness or confusion of behavior (F) and judged hostility (Jh), and the C group shows a statistically stronger reduction of depression (D) and dependency (De)

Sixteen Personality Factor Results

Table 5 summarizes the differences in changes of 16 PF scores of T and C groups. The names of scales in the table are occasionally changed to a popular term which in my opinion sums up adequately the more detailed description of a factor. The T group appears significantly more improved—without a corresponding improvement in the C group—along the dimensions described by attributes (See Appendix V):

Emotionally stable; ego strength; mature; calm; realistic—factor C.

Enterprising; active; sociable; friendly; carefree—factor H.

Flexible; oriented to problem solving—factor $Q1$ (On this factor the C group shows change in the opposite direction significant at the .001 level when compared with the T group.)

Excitability, tenseness—factor $Q4$.

The C group appears changing in two directions without significant changes in the T group:

Relaxed security; tolerance; cheerfulness—factor L
Practicality; common sense—factor M.

The C group is also more significantly improved statistically in the direction of higher self-sentiment, will power—factor $Q3$, although T group is markedly improved on it too.

On factor A (warm, sociable, kindly), the T group shows a moderately significant improvement absent in the C group.

Self and Ideal Self Results

The changes of scores on sortings are given in Table 6.

The T group subjects are statistically more improved on Deck I, and less improved on Deck III than group C on the self-concept. With regard to such improvement in self-concept, these delinquents show changes more like those in a mental hospital population than a sample of delinquent boys (Truax *et al*, 1966) who moved in the negative direction.

On the Ideal Self concept neither group shows a significant rise in scores, although group T has a lower posttherapy Ideal score on Deck II and III and group C has scores higher on all three decks. This relative relaxing about the exacting Ideal Self is considered here as a less neurotic trend with the T group.

TABLE 4

Means of *T* and *C* Groups on Clinical and Additional MMPI Scales at the Pretherapy (*Pr*) and Posttherapy (*Po*) Testing

Scale	T Pr	T Po	C Pr	C Po	Scale	T Pr	T Po	C Pr	C Po
L—lie	52.4	52.8	50.6	48.0	R—repression	14.6	16.1*	15.0	15.8
F—oddness, confusion	67.7	57.1***	63.2	57.6**	Dq—delinquency	16.0	12.4*	13.0	11.3
K—defensiveness	49.2	53.6	51.1	56.5	Cn—control	22.5	22.1	22.5	23.0
Hs—hypochondriasis	52.4	51.1	48.6	49.3	Es—ego strength	38.3	40.9	40.4	44.7***
D—depression	55.9	50.5*	51.3	46.8**	De—dependency	28.0	23.6*	30.0	21.5**
Hy—hysteria	55.9	51.1?	49.6	45.1	Do—dominance	11.8	13.1	11.5	12.1
Pd—psychopathic deviate	78.5	71.3*	73.1	69.4?	Ca—excitability	15.8	13.5**	16.1	15.2
Mf—femininity	58.7	55.0?	56.1	58.6?	Re—responsibility	15.1	15.5	15.0	16.7
Pa—paranoia	63.9	60.3	59.6	54.8	Rec—recidivism	10.4	11.1	10.7	10.6
Pt—psychasthenia	63.9	56.9?	60.4	57.9	Jh—judged hostility	19.1	15.0**	20.9	17.1*
Sc—schizophrenia	66.8	58.9**	66.4	59.9	Ho—hostility (Cook)	26.3	20.7*	27.0	20.6*
Ma—hypomania	65.4	60.6	66.4	59.1	Ad—admission of symptoms	21.1	26.1?	24.1	27.6?
Si—insecurity, shyness	57.1	52.4	59.1	53.6	Dn—denial of symptoms	11.4	12.8	11.2	13.2?
At—manifest anxiety	25.1	16.9**	21.2	16.1	So-r—social desirability	23.8	28.8***	25.4	29.7?
A—factor anxiety	20.7	13.9**	18.1	13.2?					

Differences significant at: ?p=.08; *p=.05; **p=.02; ***p=.01

140

TABLE 5

Means of *T* and *C* Groups on the Sixteen Personality Factor Questionnaire at the Pretherapy (*Pr*) and Posttherapy (*Po*) Testing

Scale	T		C		Scale	T		C	
	Pr	Po	Pr	Po		Pr	Po	Pr	Po
A—warmth	5.0	6.2?	5.6	5.4	L—suspiciousness	6.0	5.2	6.0	4.8*
B—intelligence	3.6	3.6	3.8	3.8	M—imaginativeness	5.3	5.3	5.6	4.7*
C—emotional stability	4.6	6.1**	6.1	6.7	N—shrewdness	5.0	4.8	4.8	4.7
E—dominance	4.8	4.5	4.9	4.3	O—guilt proneness	5.1	4.6	5.1	5.0
F—alertness	5.0	5.8	4.6	5.0	Q1—problem solving	4.3	6.2***	4.0	3.6
G—character	5.3	6.3	5.3	5.8	Q2—self-sufficiency	5.4	6.1	6.2	6.3
H—friendliness	3.5	5.4***	3.9	4.4	Q3—will power	4.5	6.3**	4.2	5.8***
I—sensitiveness	6.5	6.3	7.6	7.2	Q4—excitability	6.5	4.3**	4.6	3.4

Differences significant at: ?p=.08; *p=.05; **p=.02; ***p=.01

141

The main diagnostic feature sought through sortings was the discrepancy between Self and Ideal Self. The discrepancy is taken to represent the neurotic burden of self-dissatisfaction, self-rejection, and guilt. The T group shows a tentatively significant trend toward reduction in discrepancy between Self and Ideal Self on Deck I and III over the pretherapy to posttherapy period, and C group does not exhibit the trend to the same extent. The disturbing gap of what the subjects see themselves to be and what they think they ought to be becomes reduced through therapy to more reasonable proportions. The neurotic self-condemnation is decreased with the group in therapy.

TABLE 6

Means of T and C Groups on the Self and Ideal Self Sortings, and Their Discrepancies at the Protherapy (Pr) and Posttherapy (Po) Testing

Sort or Scale	T		C	
	Pr	Po	Pr	Po
Deck I, Self	24.6	32.6***	30.1	35.2**
Deck II, Self	30.3	30.3	32.9	34.5
Deck III, Self	28.0	29.3	29.2	34.2**
Deck I, Ideal Self	32.8	34.5	36.3	38.1
Deck II, Ideal Self	32.7	30.6	35.1	36.6
Deck III, Ideal Self	29.8	29.4	31.7	34.4
Deck I, discrepancy	8.2	1.9?	6.2	2.9
Deck II, discrepancy	2.4	.3?	2.3	2.1
Deck III, discrepancy	1.8	.1	2.5	.2

Differences significant at: ?p=.08, **p=.02, ***p=.01

Hostility-Guilt Index Results

Table 7 shows a significant reduction of hostility scores of the T group on the total and three subscales: assault, irritability, and verbal hostility. Apparently the therapy group had modified or sublimated hostile impulses more than the nontherapy group. The suspiciousness seems more strongly reduced in the T than in the C group. On no other scale is the C group, significantly improved except on the guilt subscale where there is a decided reduction in awareness of guilt feelings, with a moderate trend in the same direction exhibited by the T group.

TABLE 7

Means of T and C Groups on the Hostility Guilt Index Scales
at the Pretherapy (Pr) and Posttherapy (Po) Testing

Scale	T		C	
	Pr	Po	Pr	Po
Ho—total hostility	39.3	30.0**	34.4	31.0
A—assault	10.3	6.0*	5.0	4.5
B—indirect hostility	5.2	4.6	5.6	5.1
C—irritability	7.1	4.4**	5.6	5.3
D—negativism	2.8	2.3	2.0	2.1

Scale	T		C	
	Pr	Po	Pr	Po
E—resentment	4.0	3.4	3.1	3.4
F—suspicion	6.6	4.5**	5.4	4.0*
G—verbal hostility	7.6	6.1*	7.0	5.3
H—guilt	6.5	5.3†	7.2	5.9**

Differences significant at: †p=.08; *p=.05; **p=.02

143

Results of Kvaraceus Delinquency Proneness Scale

Table 8 shows the scores on the KD scale. Although there is a tendency of the *C* group to score more favorably on KD scales, i.e., lowering the plus and raising the minus scores, the differences are not statistically significant.

TABLE 8

Means of *T* and *C* Groups on the KD Proneness Scales
at the Pretherapy (*Pr*) and Posttherapy (*Po*) Testing

Scale	T		C	
	Pr	Po	Pr	Po
Plus	13.7	13.3	12.4	10.6
Minus	14.2	14.5	14.7	16.6
Total	—.5	—1.2	—2.3	—6.0

Rorschach Results

Of the numerous Rorschach hypotheses, as Table 9 indicates, only two were confirmed: the appropriate concepts ($+F\%$) are decidedly increased in *T* group, and inappropriate concepts ($-F\%$) decreased, which does not occur in the *C* group. Actually, the $-F$ concepts have increased in the *C* group, with a probability of .11. The difference in opposite trends in the *T* and *C* group, i.e., that the *T* group avoids poor percepts and the *C* group becomes more prone to show them, is reliable at .047 probability.

Another hypothesis was indirectly confirmed concerning hostility. It was hypothesized that the *T* group would have decidedly lower scores. This did not occur, but the *C* group showed higher latent hostility scores at the posttherapy testing—a difference reliable at .05 level of probability. Two of the original hypotheses, were contradicted by the results obtained: the response time on colored cards (*RTc*) and the average item per response (*T/R*) were more significantly reduced in the *C* group than in the *T* group, contrary to my hypothesis. The *New F %* was significantly heightened in both the *T* and *C* group and not only in *T* group as hypothesized.

144

TABLE 9

Means of *T* and *C* Groups on the Rorschach Indices at the Pretherapy (*Pr*) and Posttherapy (*Po*) Testing

	T		C	
	Pr	Po	Pr	Po
R	23.9	24.5	21.2	22.3
M	3.4	3.1	3.8	3.8
C	3.2	3.0	2.1	2.3
FC	.9	1.1	.7	.8
Rejection	.7	.4	.5	.3
RT gray	19.1	16.0	25.8	22.0
RT color	24.0	18.7	29.2	17.6***
RTg—RTc	−5.5	−3.0	−3.2	4.8
T/R	40.6	32.8	41.3	30.1**
F%	21.0	20.4	24.2	19.6
F+%	60.5	61.4	84.2	69.0
New F%	83.0	89.0*	86.0	91.2*
New F+%	78.4	81.5	80.0	76.6

	T		C	
	Pr	Po	Pr	Po
A%	52.0	50.4	46.7	54.1
P	6.7	7.2	6.8	7.2
P%	30.8	32.4	34.2	35.3
+F%	64.5	77.1***	73.8	73.8
—F%	21.5	12.0**	13.2	19.0
W : M	.6	1.1	.8	.7
M : FM	1.1	1.0	1.0	1.2
C + CF : FC	.6	1.1	.7	.7
H + Hd : A + Ad	.5	.7	1.3	1.3
H	3.6	3.9	5.3	5.2
RCT — anxiety	10.6	8.4	8.3	8.8
RCT — hostility	4.2	4.7	1.8	3.5*

Differences significant at: *p=.05; **p=.02; ***p=.01

It appears that the hypothesis of the research has been well confirmed by the results just reviewed. The group in therapy shows a decisive and significantly larger psychological and behavioral progress than the matched group exposed to institutional training alone. The *T* group was judged by teachers and cottage counselors to be more improved behaviorably. It was significantly improved on seventeen traits on objective tests in which the *C* group showed no consistent improvement; it showed strong trends ($p = .08$) on five more dimensions and was more decidedly improved (lower *p*) than the *C* group along four more characteristics on which the *C* group also showed a significant parallel improvement.

It is particularly important to consider directions of improvement in the *T* group because delinquents show some typical weaknesses in their personality structures and reactions to their environment. They are impulsive, excitable, highly hostile and anxious, with inappropriate behavioral responses and distorted views of themselves and of others. The reduction of pathology on scales of sociopathic trends and disregard of social conventions (*Pd*) and on delinquency (*Dq*) are highly meaningful in the treatment of young offenders. The institutional approach alone—at least in the groups measured here—does not bring about, in a consistent way, such highly desirable changes. This conclusion is confirmed through research (Jurjevich, 1966) on the effects of institutional training. Sixty-nine delinquent girls were retested on the MMPI after eight months of training, but no significant change in antisocial orientation (*Pd*) was observed. On the other hand the exposure to psychotherapy which, in this case, means a highly personalized relationship made this change in *Pd* trends possible. Psychotherapy also brought about a decided reduction in other personality deviations which may contribute to delinquent excesses, and the less individualized institutional efforts alone left the subjects relatively unchanged:

> Hostility (HGI scales: hostility, assault, verbal hostility, irritability).
> Anxiety (*A, At* of MMPI).
> Excitability (*Ca* of MMPI, i.e., behavior proper to diffuse organic brain damage; *Q4* of 16 PF).

Distorted, inaccurate, unrealistic view of environment (—F%
    of Rorschach).
Inappropriate emotionality (*Sc* of MMPI).

The *T* group has also grown in these positive directions without
a statistically confirmed growth in the *C* group:

Friendliness, responsibility (*H* of 16PF).
Emotional stability or ego strength (*C* of 16 PF).
Problem solving, readiness to explore new approaches to
    themselves and others (*Q2* of 16 PF).
Proper, adequate, realistic perception of the surrounding
    world (+F% of Rorschach).
Repression, closing off of conflicts, warding off of disturbing
    memories (*Re* of MMPI).
Heightened awareness of socially desirable traits (*So-r* of
    MMPI).

Negative developments had also taken place in the *C* group
which did not appear in the *T* group. Presumably these undesirable
personality reactions could also have taken place in the *T* group,
for it was initially more maladjusted, had it not been for psychotherapeutic intervention. The *C* group shows significant deterioration (not manifested in the *T* group) in these trends:

Latent hostility (on RCT).
Inaccurate or distorted perception of environment (—F%
    of Rorschach).

Not only is there a significant increase in inappropriate perception (—F% of Rorschach) but also there is a trend toward losing
the capacity for adequate and realistic discernment of environment (+F% of Rorschach). When these trends are compared
in the two groups, there is a loss in the *C* group significant at
the .05 level. Another deterioration in the *C* group, when compared with the improvement in the *T* group, is the loss in problem
solving and flexible approach (factor *Q1* of 16PF, significant at
.001 level). With these statistically significant improvements—or
at least arrests of further deterioration—one can consider, in a
tentative way, some of the changes which did not reach a statis-

tically acceptable magnititude but which are in the direction of greater improvement in the *T* than in the *C* group with the *C* group sometimes showing undesirable trends:

Hysteria (*Hy* of MMPI).
Psychasthenia (*Pt* of MMPI).
Femininity of interests (*Mf* of MMPI).
Warmth, kindliness (*A* of 16 PF).
Accurate, impartial, unemotional perception (*F*+% and New *F*+% of Rorschach).

Immature, uninventive fantasy (*A*% of Rorschach).
Latent anxiety (or RCT).
Workable, less self-debasing view of the actual and ideal self (discrepancy between them).

In contrast with the greater improvements in the *T* group, the *C* group shows a statistically more certain reduction in direction of:

Depression (*D* of MMPI).
Dependency (*De* of MMPI).
Will power (*Q3* of 16 PF).

There are two unambiguously desirable aspects on which the *C* group shows greater improvement than *T* group: the ego-strength scale (*Es*) of MMPI, and the suspiciousness factor (*L*) of 16 PF. The differential growth of the *C* group along *Es* scale is unexpected and contradictory to the results previously discussed. Several explanations can be offered tentatively. It is possible that the "no-nonsense-tolerated" approach of a large part of the institutional staff creates an awareness of reality demands more sharply than the more permissive and psychologically-oriented approach of the psychotherapist. The nontherapy girls may have been made more watchful as to "proper" behavior. These reality-bound trends can be seen in their lowered scores on the imaginativeness (*M*) scale of 16 PF in the direction of practicality; in the decidely higher Self and Ideal Self estimates; in the higher denial of symptoms scale (*Dn* of MMPI); in higher apprehensiveness, anxiety, and hostility which would naturally appear in a strict setting.

The *Es* scale may also not be fully valid for an adolescent and delinquent population because it was standardized for an adult, neurotically disabled population. The partial validity of *Es* for the subjects of this research can be indicated by the opposite results obtained on a similarly named scale, namely, *C* scale of 16 PF (emotional stability or ego strength) on which the *T* group is decidedly more improved. Another possible explanation is to be found in the incomplete nature of psychotherapy described herein. The relatively small number of interviews might have the effect of resolving some ego defenses and creating a number of breaches in the traditional personality adjustment that makes the subjects less bound to the hard aspects of reality. Among all these possible explanations, I choose the one that the *Es* scale is not valid for the population to which it was applied. Investigating the short term test-retest reliability of MMPI scales (Jurjevich, 1966a), I have found the *Es* scale significantly improved on the retest after ten to thirty days of living in the institution. Such improvement being unlikely, the *Es* can be considered an unreliable and invalid scale. The *Es* scale apparently encourages defensive responses. It is highly correlated with the social desirability scale, *So-r*, Pearson *r* being .62 for this population, significant at $p = .001$. The *Es* scale also was found unreliable in an investigation with male Air Force personnel, after a test-retest period of eleven days (Jurjevich, 1966b).

The larger reduction of suspiciousness in the nontherapy group, as shown on factor *L* of 16 PF, is not easy to explain. It contradicts the reduction of anxiety and hostility in the *T* group, evident on other scales of anxiety and hostility, and is also contrary to the indications of the factors *A* (warmth) and *F* (friendliness) of 16 PF and of scale *F* (suspicion) of HGI. A tentative explanation for the lesser reduction in jealousy and possessiveness of Factor *L* in the *T* group may be the result of the personalized relationship in therapy and the shortness of the therapeutic process which may have only begun for some girls by the time they were retested.

There are some changes in the *C* group whose meaning does not appear clear when their absence is noted in the *T* group. One such change is on the Guilt Scale of HGI. I take the view that reduction of conscious guilt feelings is not a healthy development in the *C* group, and is more likely to be a self-deluding attempt than a genuine inner comfortableness; they have repressed guilt feelings instead of resolving them through appropriate

149

activity, because they are not seen as behaving better by teachers and cottage personnel and have not come to be less hostile or anxious. Their reduction in guilt feelings is likely to be spurious. Lack of corresponding improvement on the guilt-proneness scale (O of 16 PF) lends further validity to this viewpoint.

Two other ambiguous changes in the C group are on the reaction time to colored cards (RTc) and response time (T/R) on Rorschach. These indices have not been claimed to be stable personality variables in the Rorschach literature; their meaning is considered relative to other personality manifestations on a Rorschach test. Prior to research my assumption was that a shorter RTc would mean a lessened proneness to upsets on emotional impacts, and shorter T/R would mean improved mental efficiency as manifested in straightforward responses. These meanings can hardly be considered tenable for the C group, in view of the preponderant evidence of its poorer status on large numbers of better validated scales.

The likelihood of obtaining by chance significant results on the test scales by simply increasing the number of scales used was also investigated. On none of the tests, except Rorschach, does the number of significant differences appear as a result of chance. The probability that the number of significantly improved scores from pretherapy to posttherapy could have arisen by chance is smaller than .0002, making it highly unlikely (Wilkinson, 1951). For Rorschach, such probability is .127 for the T group, and .034 for the C group, reducing the decisiveness of the Rorschach findings.

Conclusions

The implications of this research bear upon several important problems which have not been systematically investigated up to now.

First, the research results point to the feasibility of treating adolescent delinquent girls, particularly when psychotherapy is offered to those who are confined and trained in modified traditional institutions. There can be no doubt that delinquent girls can benefit from individual psychotherapy. The opinions to the contrary that character disorders are unlikely to yield to psychotherapy may be due to the contaminating effects of different institutional setups, or the different expectations and attitudes of the

150

therapists, or different methods used and goals established for psychotherapy.

Second, the relative lack of improvement behaviorally and psychologically in the control group, and the appearance of some undesirable trends indicate that the institutional approach alone is insufficient to cause many desirable changes in the attitudes of delinquents. These changes can be effected with more severely disturbed youngsters through the personalized approach of workers trained to deal with emotional deviations and personality misdevelopments.

Third, the rigidity of institutional patterns need not detract from the effectiveness of individual psychotherapy. This is an important understanding, for psychotherapists need not wait for the slow institutional changes to occur before they can effectively treat youngsters committed to an institution. It is my definite impression that the institutional pressures and irritations have raised the level of anxiety and hostility in the subjects and forced them to utilize psychotherapy with greater eagerness.

Fourth, psychotherapeutic effects with delinquents can be achieved by moderately-trained professional personnel if they use the method employed by me in this research. The therapy of delinquents need not be postponed until institutions are able to employ recognized medical or nonmedical specialists in psychotherapeuitc procedures. Genuine interest in helping delinquents—which I consider the principal therapeutic agent here—may make up for the lack of specific or advanced training in psychotherapy, provided that the therapist is capable of informed and mature handling of his subjects.

Fifth, there is no necessity to look for help only to psychiatrists; they are in too short supply. There is no exclusive need for medically-trained psychotherapists to treat some of the seriously aberrant delinquents, because they can be treated effectively by clinical psychologists and psychiatric social workers who are more numerous and more available to institutions. Persons (1966) reports that five of the therapists in his research project (two psychologists, and three-relatively inexperienced social workers) showed no significant difference—as professional groups—in the results they obtained through psychotherapy, although the psychologists' subjects showed slightly greater improvement trends.

Sixth, psychotherapy may not be the answer to all the adjustment problems of institutional delinquents. Some of them do not respond to therapy, or their treatment absorbs an exorbitant amount of time with relatively meager returns, as is obvious from some of the cases I have described in Part I. The subjects should be carefully selected.

Seventh, psychological tests appear to be feasible instruments for measuring psychological change. This possibility seems to have been dismissed even by psychologists themselves, as evidenced by an American Psychological Association publication (Rubinstein and Parloff, 1959).

Eighth, considering the lack of significant personality test improvements by both predelinquent young boys (Powers and Witmer, 1951), delinquent boys (Truax, *et al.*, 1966), and young men offenders (Rudoff and Bennet, 1958), it may be hypothesized that adolescent girls are more amenable to psychotherapeutic influence and to institutional training (Jurjevich, 1966a).

Ninth, the results obtained provide a rough verification of the efficiency of psychotherapy not based wholly on the prevalent Freudian or nondirective approaches. The method employed was less searching into the past of the subjects than "psychodynamic" theory might require, and was more directive than the client-centered approach considered appropriate. The method contained personal reacting on the part of the therapist and in some respects, was akin to psychotherapeutic teaching.

Tenth, the research described here represents only an approximation to a final and systematic verification of the effects of therapy on delinquent girls. Several extensions and improvements in the present design are necessary before the question could be answered with enough definiteness to generalize on the wider field of treatment of delinquent girls in institutions. The exposure to psychotherapy should be longer. It can be postulated that therapy for some of the girls had only begun, when it was interrupted after twenty interviews and measurements taken.

At best, the therapy evaluated here is of the short-term variety. A larger number of interviews could presumably consolidate and intensity the changes begun in the sessions evaluated herein. A more decisive experiment might also include a larger number of subjects and several therapists; male delinquents should be included in the extended research design as well as therapists of different sex and age; psychotherapists of different backgrounds, levels of training, and experiences (psychiatrists, clinical psychologists, social workers, pastors, and educators) also should be tried to test their relative effectiveness with delinquents. Different psychotherapeutic systems could be applied: reality therapy, integrity therapy, relaxation methods, hypnosis, et cetera. A larger number of tests and rating scales included in the evaluative criteria as well as recordings of interviews would prove of value, with a follow-up study of subjects carried out after a year—a study that would repeat the tests and ratings used in the experiment proper as well as provide other rating schedules as reported here.

When all these necessary extensions are considered it is obvious that the present research is only an exploratory study for wider investigative efforts.

Follow-up Study

Two years after termination of therapy both T and C group subjects were rated for parole adjustment by the parole agents supervising the individual girls. By the time of rating, all subjects had been released on parole for at least a year.

I have devised a Rating Schedule of Parole Adjustment (RSPA, Appendix VII). There were 6 raters, some rating only one subject, some 11. The items 4,5,7,8,9,10 of RSPA were scored 1-5, the lowest number being used for the least desirable rating. Item 3, staying on parole, was considered to be the resultant of all other aspects of adjustment rated by items 4-10. Assuming that the average rating on these 6 items could be 2.5, the satisfactory remaining on parole was scored 15. If the parolee had to be returned to the institution, or had escaped from placement and was out of reach of parole agents, the score assigned to item 3 was zero.

Item 6, about the helpfulness of placement, was also considered to be influential in the overall parole adjustment and to pervade the personality reactions rated on items 4,5,7-10. The scores on item 6 were used in weighting the total score of the Schedule. The weight of zero was given to the rating of the placement as most helpful. If the rating of placement was as "quite detrimental" (none fell in this category), the weight assigned was 16. The scores for other ratings were: "not very helpful," 12, "indifferent," 8, and "mildy helpful," 4.

153

TABLE 10

Sums of Ratings of the T and C Groups on Rating Schedule of Parole Adjustment

Item	Sum of Ratings	
	T	C
3. Staying on parole	166	136
4. Responsibility at placement	46	46
5. Maturity of behavior (adult estimate)	43	43
6. Helpfulness of placement	100	76
7. Effort at adjustment	50	51
8. Attitude toward parole agent	54	54
9. Emotional stability (agent's estimate)	50	47
10. Benefit from training	45	43
Sum, Items 3-10	554	491
Sum, Items 4,5,7-10	286	279

Table 10 summarizes the results of parole ratings. None of the differences are statistically significant. In a rigorous view the therapy and nontherapy groups do not appear to parole agents to differ appreciably in the ways they had behaved when they left the institution and were still on parole. Such a rigorous interpretation leaves out of account an important consideration, namely, that the T group was initially more maladjusted than the C group. The T Group was rated by teachers and counselors as significantly more disturbed, was more unconsciously anxious and hostile, and showed more delinquent characteristics on MMPI. Other initial scores on psychopathological trends of the T group were mostly higher on negative and lower on positive characteristic without reaching a statistical significance, as can be seen from Table 2.

If it were possible to use the HOW for ratings by teachers,

parents, or workhome adults, perhaps, the T group would have shown a continuous behavioral improvement on parole and developed the trend noted by institutional teachers and counselors in their posttherapy ratings. Such a procedure was not possible because I had left the correctional system.

Without being able to take into systematic account the initial level of maladjustment of the subjects in comparing their behavior on parole, we can only resort to speculation. It appears that psychotherapy might be considered as one of the influences helping the more disturbed T group handle the parole conditions as well or better than the less severely maladapted C group. This relative equality of adjustment is more impressive when we see that the placement of T group subjects was considerably less helpful than that of the C group. Nevertheless, only two of the girls in the T group broke their parole as compared with four in the C group.

In summary, the parole adjustment of the T group was not reliably better than that of the C group, although the ratings favor the group of girls who were in therapy.

It is of interest that 9 of the girls who had therapy married within two years, and only 3 of the nontherapy group did so. It can be speculated that therapy encouraged the girls to be more comfortable in interpersonal relationships, and made it easier for them to assume family responsibilities. Two of the C group girls ran away with men, without marrying. None of the T group did so.

Summary

The hypothesis to be verified by the present research is that the individual psychotherapy of institutionalized delinquent girls brings about a greater psychological improvement than institutional training alone.

There were 14 girls in therapy, with an average of 23 interviews. They were administered 6 psychological tests prior to, and after therapy. A behavior rating schedule was completed by teachers and cottage counselors on each girl. The same procedure was used for a matched control group of 14 subjects. The therapy group was somewhat more maladjusted to begin with. There was only one therapist. The method and other variables affecting psychotherapy are described in detail.

The therapy group showed significant improvement in the

following scales, but the control group did not reach significant changes on them: behavioral ratings of teachers and counselors; psychopathic deviate; perception of socially desirable traits; schizophrenic trends; manifest anxiety; *A* factor anxiety; delinquency; tenseness; excitability; repression; emotional stability; alertness; friendliness; problem solving; hostility; assault; irritability; suspicion; verbal hostility; adequate perception; distorted perception. The control group showed larger improvement on scales of suspiciousness and ego strength of MMPI. However, the latter scale appears to be of doubtful validity. The control group showed deterioration on: problem solving; realistic perception; inappropriate perception; guilt feelings; latent hostility.

The follow-up after two years shows trends toward a slightly better parole adjustment by the therapy group.

In conclusion, several implications were discussed: treatability of delinquents; the contribution of institutional practices to psychotherapy; psychotherapeutic personnel; and possible lines of extension of the research design.

REFERENCES

1. Aichhorn, A. *Wayward Youth* (New York: Meridian Books, 1955.)
2. Allport, G. W. *Becoming: Basic Considerations for a Psychology of Personality* (New Haven: Yale University Press, 1955.)
3. Beukenkamp, Jr., C. *Fortunate Strangers: An Experience in Group Psychotherapy* (New York: Grove Press, 1958).
4. Bilmes, M. "The Delinquent's Escape from Conscience," *Amer. J. Psychother.,* 1965, 19, pp. 633-640.
5. Boring, E. G. "Was This Analysis a Success? Symposium: Psychoanalysis as Seen by Analyzed Psychologists," *J. Abnorm. Soc. Psychol.,* 1940, 35, pp. 150-175.
6. Buehler, R. E., Patterson, G. R., and Furniss, J. "The Reinforcement of Behavior in Institutional Settings," *Behav. Res. Ther.,* 1966, 4, pp. 157-167.
7. Buss, A. H., and Durkee, Ann. "An inventory for Assessing Different Kinds of Hostility," *J. Consult. Psychol.,* 1953, pp. 21, 343-349.
8. Cattell, R. B., Saunders, D. R., and Stice G. *Handbook for*

the Sixteen Personality Factor Questionnaire. Forms A, B, and C. Champaign. III.: Institute for Personality and Ability Testing, 1957.

9. Corsini, R., and Uehling, H. F. "Cross Validations of Davidson's Rorschach Score," *J. Consult. Psychol.,* 1954, 18, pp 277-279.

10. Davidson, Helen H. "A Measure of Adjustment Obtained from the Rorschach Protocol," *J. proj. Tech.,* 1950, 14, pp. 31-38.

11. Eissler, K. R. (Ed.) *Searchlights on Delinquency: New Psychoanalytic Studies* (New York: International Universities Press, Inc., 1949).

12. Eissler, K. R. "Some Problems in Delinquency," in Eissler, K. R. (Ed.) *Searchlights on Delinquency: New Psychoanalytic Studies* (New York: International Universities Press, Inc., 1949b).

13. Elizur, A. "Content Analysis of the Rorschach, with Regard to Anxiety and Hostility," *J. Proj. Tech.,* 1949, 13, pp. 247-284.

14. Ellis, A. "Outcome of Employing Three Techniques of Psychotherapy," *J. Clin. Psychol.,* 1957, 13, pp. 344-350.

15. Eysenck, H. J. "The effects of Psychotherapy: An evaluation," *J. Consult. Psychol.,* 1952, 16, pp. 319-326.

16. Eysenck, H. J. "The Effects of Psychotherapy," in Eysenck, H. J. (Ed.) *Handbook of Abnormal Psychology: An Experimental Approach* (New York: Basic Books, Inc., 1961).

17. Eysenck, H. J. "The Outcome Problem in Psychotherapy: A reply," *Psychotherapy,* 1964, 1, pp. 97-100.

18. Forer, B. R., Farberow, N. L., Feifel, H., Meyer, M. M., Sommers, Vita S., and Tolman, Ruth S. "Clinical Perception of the Therapeutic Transaction," *J. Consult. Psychol.,* 1961, 25, pp. 93-101.

19. Fries, Margaret E. "Some Points in the Transformation of a Wayward to a Neurotic Child," in Eissler K. R. (Ed.) *Searchlights on Delinquency: New Psychoanalytic Studies.* (New York: International Universities Press, Inc., 1949).

20. Glasser, W. *Mental Health or Mental Illness? Psychiatry for Practical Action* (New York: Harper, 1960).

21. Glasser, W. "Reality Therapy—A new approach," invited

presentation at the 32nd Annual Governors Conference on Youth, Chicago, May 10, 1963. Mimeographed.

22. Glover, E. "The Therapeutic Effect of Inexact Interpretation," *Int. J. Psychoan.*, 1931, 12. Cited by Fernichel, O. *The Psychoanalytic Theory of Neurosis* (New York: Norton, 1945), p. 565.

23. Goldstein, K. "The Organismic Approach," in Arieti, S. (Ed.) *American Handbook of Psychiatry* (New York: Basic Books, Inc., 1959), Vol. II.

24. Hill, B. "An Experiment in Treating Seriously Disturbed Juvenile Delinquent Boys," *Psychiat. Quart. Supplem.*, 1953, 27, pp. 105-119.

25. Haggerty, M. E., Olson, W.C., and Wickman, E. K. *Haggerty-Olson-Wickman Behavior Rating Schedules: Scales for the study of behavior problems and problem tendencies in children* (New York: World Book Company, 1930).

26. Jurjevich, R. M. "The Effects of Ego-inflating and Ego-deflating Responses of the Psychotherapist," Doctoral Dissertation, University of Denver, 1958. Unpublished.

27. Jurjevich, R. M. "Normative Data for the Clinical and Additional MMPI Scales for a Population of Delinquent Girls," *J. Gen. Psychol.*, 1963, 69, pp. 143-146.

28. Jurjevich, R. M. "Personality Changes Concomitant with Institutional Training of Delinquent Girls," *J. Gen. Psychol.*, 1966a, 74, pp. 207-216.

29. Jurjevich, R. M. "Short Interval Test-retest Stability of MMPI, California Psychological Inventory, Cornell Index and a Symptom Check List," *J. Gen. Psychol.*, 1966b, 74, pp. 201-206.

30. Jurjevich, R. M. "The Regression Toward Mean in MMPI, California Psychological Inventory and Symptom Check List," *Educ. Psychol. Measmt.*, 1966c, 26, pp. 661-664.

31. Klopfer, B., Ainsworth, M. D., Klopfer, W.G., and Holt, R. R. *Developments in the Rorschach Technique: Technique and Theory,* (Yonkers-on-Hudson, N.Y.: World Book Co., 1954).

32. Knopf, I. J. "Current Status of the Rorschach Test," Symposium 1955, 4. "The Rorschach Test and Psychotherapy," *Am. J. Orthopsychiat.*, 1956, 26, pp. 801-806.

33. Kvaraceus, W. C. *KD Proneness Scale and Check List:*

Manual of Directions (rev.) (New York: World Book Co., 1953).

34. Lampl-De Groot, Jeanne, "Neurotics, Delinquents and Ideal-formation," in Eissler, K. R. (Ed.), *Searchlights on Delinquency: New Psychoanalytic Studies* (New York: International Universities Press, Inc., 1949).

35. Levitt, E. E. "The Results of Psychotherapy with Children: An Evalutaion," *J. Consult. Psychol.*, 1957, 21, pp. 189-196.

36. Lippman, H. S. "Difficulties Encountered in the Psychiatric Treatment of Chronic Juvenile Delinquents," in Eissler, K. R. (Ed.), *Searchlights on Delinquency: New Psychoanalytic Studies* (New York: International Universities Press, Inc., 1949).

37. Morse, P. N. "Psychotherapy with the Non-reflective Aggressive Patient," *Am. J. Orthopsychiat.*, 1958, 28, pp. 352-361.

38. Mowrer, O. H. *The Crisis in Psychiatry and Religion* (New York: D. Van Nostrand, Co., Inc., 1961).

39. Mowrer, O. H. *The New Group Therapy* (New York: D. Van Nostrand, Co., Inc., 1964).

40. Nacht, S. "The Curative Factors in Psychoanalysis," Part II. *Int. J. Psychoanal.*, 1962, 43, pp. 206-211.

41. Persons, R. W. "Psychological and Behavioral Changes in Delinquents Following Psychotherapy," *J. Clin. Psychol.*, 1966, 22, pp. 337-340.

42. Persons, R. W. "Relationship Between Psychotherapy with Institutionalized Boys and Subsequent Community Adjustment," *J. Consult. Psychol.*, 1967, 31, pp. 137-141.

43. Pfister, O. "Therapy and Ethics in August Eichhorn's Treatment of Wayward Youth," in Eissler, K. *Searchlights on Delinquency: New Psychoanalytic Studies* (New York: International Universities Press, Inc., 1949).

44. Powers, E. and Witmer, Helen, *An Experiment in the Prevention of Delinquency: The Cambridge-Somerville Youth Study* (New York: Columbia University Press, 1951).

45. Rapaport, D. *Diagnostic Psychological Testing* (Chicago: The Yearbook Publishers, 1946), Vol. II.

46. Rogers, C. R. "Toward a Science of the Person," in Wann, T. W. (Ed.), *Behaviorism and Phenomenology* (Chicago: University of Chicago Press, 1964).

47. Rogers, C. R., Kell, W. L., and McNeal, H. "The Role of Self-understanding in the Prediction of Behavior. *J. Consult. Psychol.,* 1948, 12, pp. 174-186.
48. Rogers, C. R. and Dymond, Rosalind F. *Psychotherapy and Personality Change* (Chicago: University of Chicago Press, 1954).
49. Rubinstein, E. A. and Parloff, M. B. *Research in Psychotherapy* (Washington D.C.: American Psychological Association, Inc., 1959).
50. Rudoff, A. *The PICO Project: A Measure of Case Work in Corrections,* Second Technical Report of Preliminary Findings (Tracy, California, California State Department of Corrections, Deuel Vocational Institution, 1959).
51. Schmideberg, Melitta, "The Borderline Patient," in Arieti, S. (Ed.), *American Handbook of Psychiatry* (New York: Basic Books, 1959).
52. Schwartz, L. J. "Treatment of the Adolescent Psychopath: Theory and Case Report," *Psychotherapy,* 1967, pp. 4, 133-137.
53. Seguin, C. A. *Love and Psychotherapy: The Psychotherapeutic Eros* (New York: Libra Publishers, Inc., 1965).
54. Shelley, E. L. V., and Johnson, W. F. "Evaluation as Organized Counseling Service for Youthful Offenders," *J. Counsel. Psychol.,* 1961, 8, 351-354.
55. Shulman, I. "The Dynamics of Certain Reactions of Delinquents to Group Psychotherapy," *Int. J. Gp. Psychother.,* 1952, 2, pp. 333-343.
56. Siegel, S. *Nonparametric Statistics for the Behavioral Sciences* (New York: McGraw-Hill. Inc., 1956).
57. Slavson, S. R. *The Practice of Group Therapy* (New York: International Universities Press, Inc. 1947).
58. Small, L. *Rorschach Location and Scoring Manual* (New York: Grune & Stratton, Inc., 1956).
59. Sohn, L. "Group Therapy of Young Delinquents," *Brit. J. Delinq.,* 1952, 3, pp. 20-33.
60. Stevenson, I. "The Challenge of Results in Psychotherapy," *Amer. J. Psychother.,* 1959, 116, pp. 120-123.
61. Truax, C. B. "Effects of Group Therapy with High Accurate Empathy and Non-possessive Warmth Upon Female

Institutionalized Delinquents," *J. Abnorm. Psychol.*, 1966, 71, pp. 267-274.

62. Truax, C. B., and Carkhuff, R. R. "Client and Therapist Transparency in the Psychotherapeutic Encounter," *J. Counsel. Psychol.*, 1965, 12, pp. 3-9.

63. Truax, C. B., Carkhuff, R. R., Wargo, D. G., Kodman, F., and Moles, E. A. "Changes in Self-concepts During Group Psychotherapy as a Function of Alternate Sessions and Vicarious Therapy Pretraining in Institutionalized Mental Patients and Juvenile Delinquents," *J. Consult. Psychol.*, 1966, 30, pp. 309-314.

64. Watt, G. D. "An Evaluation of Non-directive Counseling in the Treatment of Delinquents," *J. Educ. Res.*, 1949, 42, pp. 343-352.

65. Welsch, E. E. Discussion of Chapters, I, II, III, in Balser, B. H. (Ed.), *Psychotherapy of the Adolescent* (New York: International Universities Press, Inc., 1957).

66. Wilkinson, B. "A Statistical Consideration in Psychological Research," *Phychol. Bull.*, 1951, 48, pp. 156-158.

67. Wortis, J. *Fragments of an Analysis with Freud* (New York: Simon and Schuster, Inc., 1954).

APPENDICES

Appendix I

Questionnaire Regarding Interest in Individual Psychotherapy

Date .... Your name ....

Questionnaire about your desiring or not desiring the counseling

Some of you already know what psychological counseling is. It is a way of getting help with troubles one may feel within oneself or in living with others. Through talking with a counselor about things that make you unhappy or tense, angry or fearful, confused or desperate, you may come to understand some of the reasons for such upsetting feelings and become able to handle yourself in a more successful way. The counselor does not tell you what's wrong with you, or what you have to do. You make your own findings and conclusions, with the counselor helping you only occasionally. Whatever you tell your counselor has to remain strictly confidential, so that you can talk without any fear.

This questionnaire is meant to obtain only an impression about what your attitude to counseling is. At present *we do not have* enough trained psychological counselors in our institution to make it possible for every girl to be in counseling if she so desires. However, we shall try to offer the opportunity to as many girls as possible. Let us also assure you that no girl would be made to take part in counseling. It is completely voluntary, and you can refuse to start or may discontinue your counseling sessions any time you like.

We want you to feel completely free to mark this questionnaire in the box marked *NO* if you feel that you would not care to talk with a counselor about your feelings or troubles. If you feel that you would like to try it, provided there is an opportunity, mark the box with *YES* on it. Thank you.

NO   YES

Appendix II

The Rationale of the Rorschach Hypotheses

A. Indices expected to be higher (more improved) with T than C group:

1. Number of responses, R

Some studies indicate that R is correlated with staying in therapy, presumably with progress in therapy.

2. Good form responses, $F+\%$

The more accurate, affectively not distorted, responses can be expected in stabilized perceptual functions.

3. Human movement, M

Usual interpretations of this sign are that it represents a mature, creative relationship to reality.

4. Form-color responses

These are considered as indices of capacity to respond socially appropriately in affect-arousing situations.

5. Adequate, appropriate percepts, $+F\%$

Accurate, consensually valid precepts are a sign of satisfactory reality testing.

The $+F$ percepts were determined by refering a concept to the ratings of Small's (1956) Manual. If not found in Small, only occasionally the case, I relied on my own evaluation of the concept.

The $+F\%$ embrace all categories of accurate responses, with the form primary or subordinate. The $F+\%$ responses refer only to accurate responses where only the form is evident.

6. Human content responses $H\%$

The increased accessibility of human content associations is taken as reduction in interpersonal and intrapersonal conflicts.

7. New form responses, *New $F\%$*

Representing all the responses in which the form is predominant, the increase in *New F%* should be concomitant with a rise of ego mastery over impulsive affective trends.

The *New F%* was introduced by Rapaport (1946, p. 186-187)

8. New form responses, accurate or appropriate, *New F+%*
These responses should even more represent a proper perception of reality, for they include only the *New F* percepts with "good" form.

9. Human to animal movement ratio, *M:FM*
A larger proportion of *M* in relationship to *FM* is taken to indicate the prevalence of mature over immature fantasy.

The following scale was used for scoring the *FM:M* ratio:

3.6 or higher, or if M = O or FM = O	— 0 points
2.6 — 3.5	— 1 point
1.6 — 2.5	— 2 points
.5 — 1.5	— 3 points

10. Form-color to Color-form ratio, *FC:CF + C*
The higher *FC* in the ratio is considered a sign of ego mastery over affective predominance.

The scales used in scoring the *C + CF:FC* ratio was:

3.6 or higher; also 0:0, also FC=0, CF=1 or more	0 points
2.6 — 3.5; also FC=1, CF=0 or 1	1 point
0—.4 or 1.6—2.6 also F—2 or more, CF—0 or 1	2 points
0.5 — 1.5	3 points

11. Human to animal content ratio, (H+Hd): (A+Ad)
The higher human content associations in the ratio are believed to represent a maturer, more self-accepting trend in personality.

The scoring scale for the ratio (A+Ad):(H+Hd) is:

3.6 or more	0 points
2.6 — 3.5	1 point
1.6 — 2.5	2 points
0.0 — 1.5	3 points
If H + Hd is larger than A + Ad	4 points

12. Higher popular percepts, P and $P\%$

The ability to perceive popular, conventional percepts is considered a sign of more appropriate reality testing.

B. Indices expected to be lower (less pathology indicated) with T than C group.

13. Number of rejections, Rej

In reevaluating the validity of the Davidson (1950) signs of adjustment, Corsini and Uehling (1954) found that only a smaller number of rejections held for better-adjusted individuals.

14. Shading scores combined.

The appearance of any of the shading scores c, K and k, whether the form was predominant or subordinate, were taken as consequences of anxiety which should be reduced with therapy.

15. Inadequate, inappropriate percepts, $-F\%$

This is the reverse of hypothesis 5 as above.

16. Whole percepts to human movement ratio, $W: M$

A too high W in the ratio is considered to represent unrealistic striving and poor utilization of inner resources.

The scoring scale for this ratio was:

3.6 or more; also M=0	0 points
2.6 — 3.5; also 0-1.5	1 point
1.6 — 2.5	2 points

17. Responses to gray and colored cards and difference between them.

A more stable mastery over affects and impulses is expected to be revealed in shorter, i.e., less "shocked" responses to gray and colored cards, as well in a smaller time difference in responding to colored and gray cards.

18. Percepts with animal content, $A\%$

The lowered $A\%$ is considered an index of maturing fantasy and livelier inner state which lead away from the "easy," superficial percepts.

19. Average time for responses, T/R

A less conflicted mind can be expected to be less vacilating and more efficient, therefore the time taken to produce a response would be lowered.

166

Appendx III

Additional Rorschach Content Test Scoring Items

In addition to Elizur's (1949) items, the RCT scores in this study were arrived at by scoring these percepts:

Hostility, h (1 point)

Dead animal; dead insect; fat man (woman); claws; making a face; sticking tongue out at me; torn objects; animal horns; animal or insect chewing; termites.

Anxiety, A (2 points)

Octopus; earthquake; girl lost in woods; gorilla; devil; rocks falling upon; hands reaching to choke you; ghostly eyes; landside; explosion; prison; tarantula; black widow spider.

Anxiety, a (1 point)

Blood; men falling away; being trapped; owl; crocodile; alligator; eyes staring at you; helpless animal; bones; spinal cord; dinosaur; flame; weird bugs; firecracker; shadows; strange animal; X-ray; tunnel.

AH (2 points each)

Woman kidnapped; robbers; cannibals; wild beast; tigers; shark.

ah (1 point each)

Eagle; skinned cat; Indians; someone nagging, electric eel.

A and h (A, 2 points; h, 1 point)

Monster; dragon; scorpion; sting ray; wolves; cyclone coming down.

Appendix IV

Self and Ideal Self Sort:

(1) Development, (2) Instructions, (3) Items

(1) The following Notes illustrate the framework within which the raters were asked to do their rating.

Notes to Raters
of the Q Sort Statements of Delinquent Girls

The Purpose of the Sort

The Q sort is to be used as one of the instruments for measuring the changes of self-concepts of girls in the State Training School. The sort is to be used along with the MMPI, Cattell's Sixteen Personality Factor Questionnaire, Rorschach, Kvaraceus Delinquency Proneness, and a rating scale. Both the girls participating in individual interviews and the matched individuals who are exposed only to the training schedule would be given the battery of tests at pretherapy and posttherapy points. The research is intended to evaluate the contributions of individual therapy over and above the benefits of other institutional influences.

The items classed in Healthy and Maladaptive categories will be used to create two or possibly three Q sorts of 50 items each. Only the items placed in the healthy or maladaptive categories by at least three of the four raters will be used in the final Q sort.

The Source of the Sort

The items of the Q sorts have been picked out from notes of over 700 interviews the psychologist held with more than 30 STS girls in the last twelve months, except for 14 statements taken from Hartley-Butler sorts. The items are constructed so that they fall roughly into equal halves—those representing healthy self-concepts, and those representing a maladjusted self-picture.

The raters are asked to sort the items into three piles and place them in the envelopes marked: Healthy Self-concepts, Maladaptive Self-concepts, and (if necessary) Neutral Self-concepts, i.e., those which, in the judgment of raters, connote neither healthy nor unhealthy self-concepts.

The frame of reference in judging the items should be based on the situational and psychological structure of these institutionalized girls, committed to the School because of delinquent behavior. Some examples might help. The delinquent girls are usually impulsive, sometimes violent, disregard the interests of others and their own; are insecure, oversensitive in interpersonal situations, slavish to the immature norms of their groups, reject responsibilities and obligations, and often are driven by neurotic conflicts. Although nondelinquent girls may need to be encouraged in self-assertiveness, the delinquent youngsters have to learn how to limit their assertiveness, when social principles are involved.

Average girls may need to learn how to give up their independence in order to comply with the group, and delinquents need to learn to stand on their own instead of complying fearfully with asocial group norms. A withdrawing girl needs the incentive not to stay in her room; the delinquent should learn the value of being alone and overcome the discomfort of facing oneself. An adjusted girl should show loyalty to friends; a sign of adjustment in a delinquent may be a desire to break away from the old friends. A normal girl should be led toward self-reliance, and an impulsive delinquent would show a sign of wisdom if she checked the views others hold of some behaviors. A healthy girl should become able to oppose adults when reasonable, and a delinquent should learn reality demands of submitting to adults and identifying with social authorities.

A young girl should be dissuaded from marrying too early, although it is an indication of growth in responsibility of a delinquent if she sees that sexual pleasure should best be enjoyed within the permanency and obligations of married life. Not telling and not listening to dirty jokes may be signs of uncomfortable repression with normal girls; but with delinquents the avoidance of dirty jokes indicates growth in mature identification with form-

169

erly rejected decent social standards. Guilt feelings may be irrationally strong with an average girl, but in delinquents they are healthy signs of either developing or reappearing superego. Shyness may be a weakness in an unassertive girl, whereas it may be a strength if it appears in a delinquent.

These examples indicate that what may be signs of adjustment for normally developing girls, can be signs of maladaptation in emotionally and socially misdirected delinquents. This does not argue that there are specific dynamics in delinquent girls which set them apart psychologically from socially adapted youngsters, but it points out that there are certain kinds of behavior these girls have to achieve if they are to avoid being in conflict with demands of living in harmony with others. The Raters are asked to keep in mind the criterion of growth in socialized behavior in assigning the items to healthy, maladaptive, and neutral Q-Sort piles.

Request to Raters

1. After sorting in three piles, please recheck your sorts, for the items are quite dear to me and I would not like them to perish in accidents.

2. Feel free to suggest a clearer English wording of items by writing your version on the back of the card, possibly initialling it too.

(2a) Instructions for Card Sorting on Self

These cards have on them statements about various feelings and understandings people have about themselves. You are asked to sort them out according to your own estimate about yourself as a person. As you realize, there are no *right* or *wrong* ways in sorting the cards; various people would sort them differently, depending on what seems important or unimportant in their view of themselves.

There are *50 cards* in each pack. As you see, there are *9 boxes* on the sorting board. At the far left you will be placing the statements that are most like you, and toward the middle descriptions that are less strongly like you. In a similar way you will be placing cards that are least like you in the boxes at the far right, putting them in boxes nearer the middle not like you, but less

170

strongly so. The easiest way to do the sorting is to follow these steps:

Step 1. Divide all the cards into 3 piles.

    a. Those that are *like* you.
    b. Those that are *indifferent,* that is, which you feel are *neither like* you nor *unlike* you in any important way.
    c. Those that are *unlike* you, ;or that are *"least like you."*

Step 2. From the pile of cards that are *"like you,"* pick up 5 cards that are more strongly like you than the others. Of these 5 cards, pick up 2 that are most strongly *"like you"* and put them in the extreme left column (*column number 9*); then place the remaining 3 cards in the *column number 8.*

Step 3. Pick up 6 cards from the remaining pile of cards "like you" which seem to represent your feelings about yourself more strongly than others and put them in *column 7.*

Step 4. Place 9 cards in *column number 6* as resembling you more closely. You may have some cards left over. Place these in *column 5.* If you do not have all 9 cards remaining from the "like you" pile, pick up from the middle pile those that are to even a slight extent more like you than other cards in the middle pile.

Step 5. Now you start sorting the "least like you" pile through the same steps as you did the *"like you" pile.* You may look again at instructions mentioned in *Steps 2 — 5.* Start with picking up the 5 cards *"least like you,"* putting 2 of these that are most *unlike* you in the last column on the right, that is *column 1.* Then place the 3 remaining cards in *column 2* and so on.

Step 6. When you are through with all the cards, check again to see that *every column* has the number of cards it should have.

Step 7. Dictate the numbers to the *tester,* then go on sorting the next set of cards.

(2b) *Instructions for Card Sorting on Ideal Self*

You have already sorted the cards about how you see yourself at present. You are now asked to sort the same sets of cards about how you would ideally like yourself to be.

The sorting method is the same as the one you have already followed in sorting the cards about your present self. That means, divide them first into 3 piles, then chose from these the 5 cards that say what you most strongly desire to be, and start placing them from the left side to the middle; then start with cards that say what you desire least to be like and place them from the extreme right column toward the middle.

(3) *Self and Ideal Self Sorting Items*

Deck 1

1. There are some important things in life, and I am ready to work hard for them.
2. Patience is one of my strong points.
3. There are things about me that other people admire.
4. I rarely feel blue.
5. I almost never have to use swear words.
6. I have a likable personality.
7. I feel strongly interested in school subjects.
8. I brought my troubles upon myself.
9. I have self-confidence.
10. Life holds many promises for me.
11. Most grown-ups have treated me right.
12. There are more good than bad points in me.
13. It's easy for me to make up my mind about most things.
14. I am sure I'll make something of myself by the time I am twenty-one.
15. As I think of myself, I get the feeling that I've been doing better in the last two or three months.
16. I usually like people.
17. I know clearly what kind of a woman I want to be in five years' time.
18. My temper is mild.
19. I prefer to make plans in advance than to let things ride.
20. I feel relaxed, and nothing really bothers me.
21. Most people have a liking for me.
22. Lately I have been able to change myself in some important ways.
23. I can hold my tongue when grown-ups anger me.
24. I can stick to the end in anything I do.
25. I almost never feel grouchy and mean.
26. I am often so tired.
27. I often hate myself.

28. When I am angry I throw things, or break them, or hit walls with my fist.
29. My feelings often draw we to do things against my reason.
30. I never feel embarrassed, no matter what I do.
31. I have scary dreams.
32. Everything bores me after a while.
33. I do not care for any of the grown-ups in this school.
34. I sometimes feel all hollow, as if life is gone out of me.
35. I wish I had never been born.
36. I often feel like crying.
37. Sometimes I am afraid, though I do not know why.
38. Even little things can upset me.
39. I do not care for anything.
40. Things seem so dead when I am being good.
41. I feel some strange restlessness in me.
42. My moods change often without obvious reason.
43. Life often seems not worth living.
44. Many thoughts swirling in my head make it hard for me to fall asleep.
45. Most matrons do not like me.
46. I rarely feel happy.
47. Sometimes I feel as if I am sitting on a volcano.
48. I can't stick with my mind to anything for more than a few minutes.
49. I am often so nervous that I could scream.
50. I sometimes wonder if my mind is all right.

Deck 2

51. It does not bother me to have my monthly periods.
52. I enjoy my meals.
53. I enjoy the work I have to do in the cottage.
54. I feel at ease when talking to grown-ups.
55. I am happier now than I was five years ago.
56. I have more on the ball than many girls I know.
57. I can stop myself if I feel like stealing something.
58. If I do not agree with what girls say or do I still try not to quarrel with them, but I hold to my opinions.
59. I almost never lie.
60. I will be able to change the bad reputation I have with people outside.

61. Most of the time I can think clearly about things.
62. I find I can obey most grown-ups.
63. It's important to me to know how I seem to others.
64. I am usually quite cheerful.
65. When girls tell me something, I do not take it as truth immediately.
66. It takes a lot to make me quarrel with a girl.
67. It seems that other girls have a lot of respect for me.
68. I ask people to show me when I do not know how to do something.
69. I am trying to please my matrons in what I do.
70. I can usually make up my mind and stick to it.
71. I do not tell dirty jokes.
72. There are at least three grown-ups in this school whom I like.
73. I have ideals about what I should be and I stick to them.
74. I usually think before I speak up.
75. Mostly I keep my promises.
76. Before I start something, I am afraid that I won't succeed.
77. Cards are stacked against me in life.
78. I often rush into things.
79. When in a crowd, I get the feeling that I do not belong.
80. It would be no fun for me to live the life of a "goodie" or a "square."
81. I enjoy being on the go all the time.
82. I wish others stopped interfering in my life.
83. I enjoy having arguments with girls.
84. I would rather go along with other girls than stick to my own ideas.
85. It seems to me that most grown-ups are just "squares."
86. I am afraid of the dark.
87. I despise myself.
88. I hate all the many rules which I have to obey.
89. Most of the grown-ups try to pick on me.
90. I think life has been too hard on me.
91. If I start wishing for something, I have to get it as soon as possible.
92. I hate girls who are "fruits" and "squares."
93. I do not think I'll ever amount to anything.
94. I am often down in the dumps.

95. If others had given me a chance, I would have had no trouble.
96. I believe I should start taking life seriously only later, when I grow older.
97. I do not care for any of the teachers here.
98. I do not want to be tied down to anything.
99. I can't warm up to anything.
100. I feel that people are putting on a show when they try to help me.

Deck 3

101. I am comfortable when talking with others.
102. I often ruin my chances.
103. I think sex can be quite beautiful.
104. I am a good mixer.
105. I enjoy having close friends.
106. There are at least a few girls here who care for me.
107. It does not bother me when matrons tell me what to do.
108. There are things about myself I am ashamed to tell anyone.
109. I can enjoy girls who are different than I.
110. There are many things in this training school which make me happy.
111. Others do not have to push me to get things done.
112. I am a hard worker.
113. I like most people with whom I come in touch.
114. I think I am basically a good person.
115. When I do something wrong, I do not start making excuses.
116. I find that religion is helping me stay good.
117. I want to be a wife and a mother as soon as possible.
118. I do carefully the work assigned to me.
119. I rarely get disgusted with people.
120. If I could live the last five years over again I would live them differently.
121. I do not care to listen to dirty jokes.
122. I quickly forget the hurts others have caused me.
123. My temper almost never gets out of control.
124. I rarely have to quarrel with others to win a point.
125. If there is some work to be done, I'd rather do it myself.
126. Things often do not seem real to me.
127. I very often feel that grown-ups are pushing me around.

128. I cannot say "no" to boys.
129. I would rather be a boy.
130. I feel uncomfortable when another girl is praised in front of me.
131. I like fellows who dare to be wild.
132. It is no use fighting the grown-ups because they win anyway.
133. I do not enjoy being with any of the girls here.
134. I feel I am a burden to others.
135. I do not have much respect for myself.
136. I get nervous and upset when someone tries to hurry me.
137. Sometimes I wish I were dead.
138. I obey only those people whom I like.
139. It does not satisfy me to stay long in love with one guy.
140. My father did not pay much attention to me.
141. I wish people would leave me alone.
142. I find that gossiping about others is a lot of fun.
143. I am a failure.
144. I do not let anyone stop me in what I want to do.
145. I am spiteful when I feel that people around me do not care for me.
146. When I want attention, I start misbehaving.
147. I am ashamed of nothing that I have ever done.
148. I can see shortcomings in most people around me.
149. I try not to think about my problems.
150. I am quite forgetful.

Appendix V

*Psychological Meaning of the Sixteen Personality Factor
Questionnaire Traits*

The Handbook (Cattell *et al.*, 1967) provides the following descriptions of the factors:

Factor A

Cyclothymia, A+ (warm, sociable)	*versus*	Schizothymia A— aloof, stiff)

This factor has been found to load most highly the following traits:

Good natured, easy going	*vs.*	Aggressive, grasping, critical
Ready to cooperate	*vs.*	Obstructive
Attentive to people	*vs.*	Cool, aloof
Softhearted, kindly	*vs.*	Hard, precise
Trustful	*vs.*	Suspicious
Adaptable	*vs.*	Rigid
Warmhearted	*vs.*	Cold

Factor B

General Intelligence, B+ (bright)	*versus*	Mental Defect, B— (dull)

The measurement of intelligence has been shown to carry with it as a factor in the personality realm some of the following ratings:

Conscientious	*vs.*	Of Lower morale
Persevering	*vs.*	Quiting
Intellectual, cultured	*vs.*	Boorish

177

Factor C

Emotional Stability or Ego Strength, C+ (mature, calm)	*versus*	Dissatisfied emotionality, C— (emotional, immature, unstable)

This factor loads:

Emotionally mature	*vs.*	Lacking in frustration tolerance
Emotionally stable	*vs.*	Changeable (in attitudes)
Calm, phlegmatic	*vs.*	Showing general emotionality
Realistic about life	*vs.*	Evasive (on awkward issues and in facing personal decisions)
Absence of neurotic fatigue	*vs.*	Neurotically fatigued
Placid	*vs.*	Worrying

Factor E

Dominance or Ascendance, E+ (aggressive, competitive)	*versus*	Submission, E— ("milk-toast," mild)

Assertive, Self-assured	*vs.*	Submissive
Independent-minded	*vs.*	Dependent
Hard, stern	*vs.*	Kindly, softhearted
Solemn	*vs.*	Expressive
Unconventional	*vs.*	Conventional
Tough	*vs.*	Easily Upset
Attention getting	*vs.*	Self-sufficient

Factor F

Surgency, F+ (enthusiastic, happy-go-lucky)	*versus*	Desurgency, F— (glum, sober, serious)

Talkative	*vs.*	Silent, introspective
Cheerful	*vs.*	Depressed
Serene, happy-go-lucky	*vs.*	Concerned, brooding
Frank, expressive	*vs.*	Uncommunicative, smug
Quick and alert	*vs.*	Languid, slow

178

Factor G

Character or Superego Strength, G+ (conscientious persistent)	versus	Lack of Rigid Internal Standards, G— (casual, undependable)
Persevering, determined	vs.	Quitting, fickle
Responsible	vs.	Frivolous
Emotionally mature	vs.	Demanding, impatient
Consistently ordered	vs.	Relaxed, indolent
Conscientious	vs.	Undependable
Attentive to people	vs.	Obstructive

Factor H

Parmia, H+ (Adventurous, "thick-skinned")	versus	Threctia, H— (shy, timid)
Adventurous, likes meeting people	vs.	Shy, withdrawn
Active, overt interest in opposite sex	vs.	Retiring in face of opposite sex
Responsive, genial	vs.	Aloof, cold, self-contained
Friendly	vs.	Apt to be embittered
Impulsive and Frivolous	vs.	Restrained, conscientious
Emotional and artistic interests	vs.	Restricted interests
Carefree, does not see danger signals	vs.	Careful, considerate, quick to see dangers

Factor I

Premsia, I+ (sensitive, effeminate)	versus	Harria, I— (tough, realistic)
Demanding, impatient, subjective	vs.	Realistic, expects little
Dependent, seeking help	vs.	Self-reliant, taking responsibility

179

Kindly, gentle	*vs.*	Hard (to point of cynicism)
Artistically fastidious, affected	*vs.*	Few artistic responses (but not lacking taste)
Imaginative in inner life and in conversation	*vs.*	Unaffected by "fancies"
Acts on sensitive intuition	*vs.*	Acts on practical, logical evidence
Attention-seeking, frivolous	*vs.*	Self-sufficient
Hypochondriacal, anxious	*vs.*	Unaware of physical disabilities

Factor L

Protension (paranoid tendency), L+ (suspecting, jealous)	*versus*	Relaxed Security, L— (accepting, adaptable)

Jealous	*vs.*	Accepting
Self-sufficient	*vs.*	Outgoing
Suspicious	*vs.*	Trustful
Withdrawn, brooding	*vs.*	Open, ready to take a chance
Tyrannical	*vs.*	Understanding and permissive, tolerant
Hard	*vs.*	Softhearted
Irritable	*vs.*	Composed and cheerful

Factor M

Autia, M+ (Bohemian introverted, absent-minded)	*versus*	Praxernia, M— (practical, concerned with facts)

Unconventional, Self-absorbed	*vs.*	Conventional, alert to practical needs
Interested in art, theory, basic beliefs	*vs.*	Interests narrowed to immediate issues
Imaginative, creative	*vs.*	No spontaneous creativity

180

Frivolous, immature in practical judgment	vs.	Sound, realistic, dependable, practical judgment
Generally cheerful, but occasional hysterical swings of "giving up"	vs.	Earnest, concerned or worried, but very steady

Factor N

Shrewdness, N+ (sophisticated, polished)	versus	Naivete, N— (simple, unpretentious)

Polished, socially alert	vs.	Socially clumsy and "natural"
Exact, calculating mind	vs.	Vague and sentimental mind
Aloof, emotionally disciplined	vs.	Warm, gregarious, spontaneous
Esthetically fastidious	vs.	Simple tastes
Insightful regarding self	vs.	Lacking self-insight
Insightful regarding others	vs.	Unskilled in analyzing motives
Ambitious, possibly insecure	vs.	Content with what comes
Expedient, "cuts corners"	vs.	Trusts in accepted values

Factor O

Guilt Proneness, O+ (timid, insecure)	versus	Confident Adequacy, O— (confident, self-secure)

Worrying, anxious	vs.	Self-confident
Depressed	vs.	Cheerful, resilient
Sensitive, tender, easily upset	vs.	Tough, placid
Strong sense of duty	vs.	Expedient
Exacting, fussy	vs.	Does not care
Hypochondriacal	vs.	Rudely vigorous
Phobic symptoms	vs.	No fears
Moody, lonely, brooding	vs.	Given to simple action

Radicalism, Q1+   *versus*   Conservatism of Temperament, Q1—

Factor Q2

Self-Sufficiency, Q2+   *versus*   Group Dependency, Q2—
(self-sufficient, resourceful)   (sociably group dependent)

Factor Q3

High Self-Sentiment   *versus*   Poor Self-Sentiment
Formation, Q3+   Formation Q3—
(controlled, exacting will power)   (uncontrolled, lax)

Factor Q4

High Ergic Tension, Q4+   *versus*   Low Ergic Tension, Q4—
(tense, excitable)   (phlegmatic, composed)

182

Appendix VI

Additional Matching Criteria

The control subjects were matched with therapy subjects on family background and level of delinquency.

The categories for family background were:

A. Parents separated.

B. Parents separated, and child was institutionalized for two or more years in her life.

C. Parents living together.
    The levels of delinquency were defined as follows:

Level 1 — Running away from home; truancy; temper tantrums and loss of control (assaultiveness, attempted suicide); "incorrigibility."

Level 2 — Sexual promiscuity; vandalism; robbery; burglary; bad checks.

Level 3 — Recidivism of offenses of level 2.

Appendix VII

For the parole adjustment of (name): ....
Rated by : ....
Please be as objective as possible. The rating will be kept confidential.

1. I had: .... contacts with parolee since her release from
      (number of)
   institution.

2. Was the parolee released from parole after the usual period
   of time?
   Yes............ No............
   If no, describe the reason: ....
   ....

3. Did she misbehave seriously enough on parole that you considered revocation at any time? Yes .... No ....
   If yes, what was the difficulty and final outcome? ....
   ....
   ....

4. Parolee carried the responsibility at school or place of work
   (check one):
   ....
   very poorly   poorly   fairly   satisfactorily   very
                                                        satisfactorily

5. The adults in parolee's environment (parents, teachers, em-
   ployees) thought that her behavior was:
   ....

   extremely somewhat fluctuating, fairly mature quite mature
   irresponsible immature unstable   for age   for age

6. The parolee was placed in (family, work situation—describe):
   ....
   ....

184

The influence of this placement upon her stability was:

....

quite   not very   indifferent   mildly   very helpful
detrimental   helpful   helpful

7. How eagerly did the parolee strain for better adjustment?

....

put out   lukewarm   stirred   tried   struggled hard
no effort   trial   occasionally   sincerely

8. The attitude of the parolee toward me was:

....

distrustful,   reserved,   noncommital,   obedient,   genuinely
insincere   guarded   changeable   compliant   cooperative

9. How emotionally stable was the parolee at your last contact with her?

....

extremely   rather   intermittently   rather   quite
unbalanced   unstable   stable & unstable   stable   stable

10. The benefit of institutional training for the parolee's more stable personality reaction, as seen toward the end of the parole period, was:

....

none   negligible   fair   considerable   very great